NOT HERE

Why American Democracy Is Eroding and How Canada Can Protect Itself

ROB GOODMAN

PUBLISHED BY SIMON & SCHUSTER

New York   London   Toronto   Sydney   New Delhi

SIMON &
SCHUSTER
CANADA

Simon & Schuster Canada
A Division of Simon & Schuster, Inc.
166 King Street East, Suite 300
Toronto, Ontario M5A 1J3

This Simon & Schuster Canada edition August 2023

SIMON & SCHUSTER CANADA and colophon are trademarks of Simon & Schuster, Inc.

For information about special discounts for bulk purchases, please contact Simon & Schuster Special Sales at 1-800-268-3216 or CustomerService@simonandschuster.ca.

Interior Design by Lexy East

Manufactured in the United States of America

10 9 8 7 6 5 4 3 2 1

Library and Archives Canada Cataloguing in Publication
Title: Not here : why American democracy is eroding and how Canada can protect itself / Rob Goodman.
Names: Goodman, Rob, author.
Description: Simon & Schuster Canada edition. | Includes bibliographical references and index.
Identifiers: Canadiana (print) 20230141390 | Canadiana (ebook) 20230141498 | ISBN 9781668012437 (hardcover) | ISBN 9781668012451 (EPUB)
Subjects: LCSH: Canada—Politics and government—21st century. | LCSH: United States—Politics and government—21st century. | LCSH: Political culture—Canada—History—21st century. | LCSH: Political culture—United States—History—21st century. | LCSH: Democracy—Canada—History—21st century. | LCSH: Democracy—United States—History—21st century.
Classification: LCC JL65 .G66 2023 | DDC 320.97109/05—dc23

ISBN 978-1-6680-1243-7
ISBN 978-1-6680-1245-1 (ebook)

For Louisa

Contents

There is a certain bleakness in finding hope
where one expected certainty.

—Ursula K. Le Guin

NOT HERE

Introduction

ZED

SEVERAL YEARS AGO, I DEVELOPED an intense and unrequited interest in the letter Z.

It is the one letter whose name changes at the 49th parallel. Even now, I can only read it as "zed" with effort. You've read it too now, and its sound in your mind tells you something important about who and where you are.

Z is a small hook on which I have hung an excessive weight of fear and hope. Z means that I am here. On most days being in Canada does not mean much beyond the ordinary, but there are days when I cannot read or hear or say the letter Z without a sense of stupid, unearned relief. One was the day I watched the rioters sack the Capitol on my laptop in Toronto. It was the first full pandemic winter: I remember the makeshift home office in our basement, the hum of the space heater, the snow melting on the doormat, the Capitol office where I'd worked in my twenties suddenly on the screen with friends and old coworkers inside (mercifully unhurt, it turned out). That night, the same as every night, I sang my daughters the ABC song before bed: "W, X, Y, and zed."

My family is American, and has been for generations. I come from nineteenth-century Jewish immigrants on both sides. America's democratic decline, or erosion, or backsliding—grave and heavy metaphors all—should not be my concern in anything other than a bloodless, calculative sense, a sense for the way it impinges on my new home. But countries don't let us off that easily. Hence the claustrophobic sense that, even here, I am still there, in a violent place with more violence to come. Hence my interest in the letter Z.

I would like to believe that I have landed elsewhere, a place with a more useable past and a more open future. I don't know when or if I'll begin to think of myself as Canadian. I can't predict how my three young daughters will come to think of themselves. But I know that a man with children, as the saying goes, has given hostages to fortune. I know that they are hostages to the fortune of *this* place. And so my feelings for this place, with all the compounded love and worry and frustration, are bound up with the love and worry and frustration of a parent, in a way that grows more entangled the deeper my children's roots here grow, in a way that I couldn't begin to disentangle if I tried.

There are days when I look out my window at a place that seems indistinguishable from the one I left, as if this were a civilization with no greater founding creed than the narcissism of small differences—and it seems laughable that the letter Z or the queen on the quarter could save us. And there are days when, somehow, it seems as if they might. Yet the longer I live here and the more I learn, the more it seems as if that state of uncertainty is a deep part of being Canadian. I am writing this, in part, to understand and express that uncertainty: one day, it might be my best claim to being from here.

So this book is, in part, an immigration story. It is a trivial one in the great and fraught scope of human movement. But it is mine. In the United States, I played a bit role in American politics, as a speechwriter in the House and Senate, and then I went back to school to earn my PhD. Now I teach political theory in Toronto. When I try to explain what brought me here, I first look for one of the big, capitalized nouns that dotted the immigration stories I learned growing up: Freedom, Religion, Opportunity. But in the space where the great abstract noun is supposed to be, I find only a human-size tangle of motives. There is the prosaic: a job. There is the prudential: excellent public schools, fewer guns, paid parental leave, a future in which my children are at least marginally less likely to be crushed under student debt or health care bills. And there are the motives I struggle to find words for even now, the clench in my stomach when I read the news from home, the foolish relief centred arbitrarily on the letter Z. The words that I've found to express those motives, such as they are, are here in this book.

I am writing this from a place intimately familiar to newcomers of all kinds, the place in between *there* and *here*. I want to pause in that place, to offer some advice to my adopted country while it and I are still new to one another—in the very brief period when I can still see it with eyes unclouded by familiarity. I am fully aware of my presumption in not waiting. In my defense, I can only plead urgency: political urgency, of course, but also urgency of a more personal kind—the kind that knows from experience how newness fades, habit piles up, eyes cloud over.

But if newness comes with its insights, it also comes with its confusions. For instance: Who are Canadians to me? *They* or *we*? Neither feels right. To tell Canadians what I believe *they* are and what I think *they* should do feels aloof and arrogant. More important, it feels false to our community of neighbours and friends here, people I certainly imagine sharing the first-person plural with me. And yet *we* still feels arrogant in its own right. Who am I, trailing my Americanness behind me, to tell Canadians who *we* are?

Fully aware that there is no satisfactory solution, I am making an arbitrary choice: *we*. Call it the aspirational *we*. The aspiration is simply this: that at some indefinite point in the future, it will come to be accurate.

———————

There is an orange shirt, child's size small, on a plastic clothes hanger on a hook beneath the mailbox in front of our house on a busy street. If we come home to find that it has blown off the hook on a windy day, we return it to its place. It has been hanging there since May 2021 and the discovery of the 215 bodies at the residential school in Kamloops, and I have trouble imagining the circumstances under which it would be appropriate to remove it for good. What is the calendar date on which those deaths turn into just another awful thing that happened? Having put it up, I can't find a reason to take it down—and so I replace it when it falls, dust it off, and hope for a wind vicious enough to blow it clear off our porch and down the street and make my decision for me.

Some of this, no doubt, is simply the ordinary ineptitude of anyone handling a new set of symbols for the first time. They come to our hands awkward, unwieldy, and cold, and only with time do they warm and soften to our use. Yet my sense is that this same uncertainty, or even paralysis, is not uncommon among settler-descended Canadians. Who are we, other than the people who put those bodies in the ground?

It may be that pride in one's country, any country, needs ignorance in the way that crops need shit. And so, confronted with the evidence of our enormities on this continent, some of us try to do without pride, and some of us, unable to do without it, work on perfecting our ignorance. But the possibility of being *proud* of Canada is not really the most serious thing at issue. Countries can live without pride. The damage is more fundamental than that: not to a set of feelings about this country, but to the ideas Canadians use to express this country's continued, distinctive existence, full stop.

I hope I'm not being hyperbolic; I don't think I am. If there is one theme in the literature of Canadian nationalism, it is the all-pervasive fear of being reduced to a cartographical fiction—or perhaps the fear that Canadians already are, and simply, mortifyingly, haven't noticed yet. The border is not just famously long and undefended, it is famously arbitrary, from Buffalo Point to the Peace Arch, a work of political power rather than geographic necessity, a fact that can always be revised in a way that, say, the Alps cannot. Canadian nationalism is haunted by the possibility of Canadian disappearance. Open one of the founding texts of modern Canadian nationalism, George Grant's *Lament for a Nation*, and there it is: "the impossibility of Canada." More than most nationalisms of which I am aware, Canada's is pitted against entropy itself.

Of course, these are essentially settlers' worries; but that is just my point. Historically, they have been tempered by the experience of the Indigenous nations for whom this has always been a home, rather than a place of extraction and exile—by this country's "senior founding pillar," in the words of John Ralston Saul. The inability to imagine those nations as part of *us* brings the old fears back with renewed force.

But beyond that, with the loss of willful ignorance (of which the mass graves are just a part) has come the loss of the very language with which Canadians have described, lamented, and resisted a place at the edge of an empire: the language of the colony. No one takes pride in being a colony—an exporter of commodities and of talent, a land of absentee landlords, a place whose elite wishes it were elsewhere—and yet the idea of the colony has done essential political work here, right up to the present.

Contemporary Canadians inherit that work. The language of the colony is no longer used as explicitly as it was as recently as the 1970s and '80s—but modern Canadian nationalism is nearly inconceivable without it, just as a building is inconceivable without the scaffolding that made it possible. The idea of the colony has given us our sense of distinctive existence. It has given a concrete shape to our separateness. It has organized Canadian resentments—of political interference, of foreign ownership, of the failings of our leaders, of our own failings. Harold Innis: "Canada moved from colony to nation to colony." Margaret Atwood: "We have been (and are) an exploited colony; our literature is rooted in those facts." Northrop Frye: Canada "is practically the only country left in the world which is a pure colony, colonial in psychology as well as in mercantile economics."

The idea of the colony defines our relationship to the great powers. It sets an overarching aim of our politics: to secure a meaningful freedom of action. It establishes our essential goodness in our own minds. Former prime minister Stephen Harper spoke to that sense of the colonial when he said, notoriously, that Canada has "no history of colonialism." And, true enough, Canada has never had colonies. It *is* a colony.

But who is the colonized? Until recently, the Canadian claim seems to have been that we all are. No doubt everyone concerned understood the ambiguity of a settler colony, in which the settler is the middle term between imperial metropole and dispossessed native, kissing up and kicking down by turns. And yet much of the talk of

Canada as a colony has plowed right through that ambiguity, repeating the founding equivalence of Canadian literature that Atwood summarized this way in 1972: "We are to the Americans as the Indians are to us."

The idea of Canada as a colony—capable of conflating the colonization of Indigenous land by English and French, and the colonization of Canadian culture and markets by Americans—has done wonders for our sense of ourselves. It has rendered our nationalism righteous and leftish. And it has put us in august company. Europeans and Americans have long done politics among themselves with a set of concepts drawn from their treatment of the Other—because that treatment gives us our curses and our nightmares, our imaginative stock of the very worst things that can happen.

The American Revolution would be almost inconceivable without the repeated, reechoed, obsessive language of slavery—a language that the American founders used quite literally, not as a florid metaphor, but as a word expressing, as they saw it, the actual truth of their relation to Britain. "How is it," asked Samuel Johnson, "that we hear the loudest yelps for liberty among the drivers of Negroes?" How could we not? Slave drivers knew the value of liberty uniquely, because they rose and slept amidst its absence. And in Johnson's England, schoolboys read in the *Aeneid* that the greatest empire of the ancient world was pleased to imagine that it was founded by war refugees, and that, with its pedigree of suffering, it alone could conquer mercifully.

Politics makes slaves of slave drivers and refugees

of conquerors—as if one of its aims, coeval with power and gain, is the displacement of the guilty conscience. It makes colonized of colonizers, as well. But all of this requires the silence of the actual slave, or refugee, or colonized. When that silence cracks, the metaphors crack, too.

In the last half century, Canada has been transformed by the increasing presence of Indigenous voices in the public sphere. And one of those transformative consequences has been the imploding plausibility of "colony" as a set of ideas to express Canada's separateness.

Without "slavery," the American Revolution is a tax dispute. Without "colony," we can lament the mediocrity of our leaders, or the insecurity of our intellectuals, or the saturation of our media by American news, or the domination of our markets by foreign capital. But, as much as those things matter, setting to work on them in the absence of "colony" lacks the kind of moral grandeur that can motivate intensive, self-sacrificial action on generational time scales. Making a nation from a colony is a world-historical mission; repatriating Tim Hortons, less so. Without a language to organize our discontents, they are just another set of problems—and, given the state of the world, not very pressing problems, either.

It has been clear for some time that our language for these things derived its power from a monstrous sleight of hand: that colonization was primarily something done *to* Canada, not *by* Canada. After Kamloops, the sleight of hand is undeniable. No wonder I don't know what to do with our orange shirt. No wonder we are frozen.

Historically, the Canadian fear of absorption has been compounded by the self-deprecating sense that our differences from America are trivial, that nothing much is in danger of being absorbed at all. As Northrop Frye put it: "What is resented in Canada about annexation to the United States is not annexation itself, but the feeling that Canada would disappear into a larger entity without having anything of any real distinctiveness to contribute to that entity."

On the American side, there have been powerful reasons to encourage this sense of Canada's triviality, which I'll return to. But what I want to stress now is that that claim, if it ever was true, is simply not true anymore. Canadians of an older generation could look south and see, if they squinted, a more-or-less equally democratic neighbour, louder and richer but not enormously distinct from English Canada. Canadians of this present generation look south and see something that demands our fear, something that speaks with an urgency missing from the earlier, vaguer anxieties of absorption. And this, just at the moment we have lost the words for our difference.

Set aside the many millions of Americans who celebrate what their country is becoming; among the rest, over the past decade, I've observed a diversity of personalized breaking points that I can only describe as kaleidoscopic. A photo of an immigrant boy behind chain link, draped in a foil blanket; police in riot gear smashing the head of an elderly protestor onto the concrete in Upstate

New York; the president, in a cloud of tear gas, brandishing the Bible like a weapon; Uvalde; or El Paso; or Parkland; or Tree of Life; or Las Vegas; or Charleston; or Sandy Hook.

I don't know how January 6 will be remembered, how my children will learn it in school one day: as a failure, a blip, the high-water mark of an authoritarian movement that Americans decisively rejected, beginning with the elections two years later; or as a trial run, a proof of concept, a beginning rather than an ending. But I also don't know if I'll ever see another American presidential election that both parties accept as legitimate. I do know that a majority of Republican congressional representatives voted to overturn the 2020 presidential election. I know that, even in the midst of a disappointing midterm for their party, some two hundred election-denying Republicans were elected to federal office. I know that nineteen states responded to the election of a Democratic president by rolling back voting rights. I know that politicians have long been in the practice of selecting their own voters for House elections, that the algorithms helping them to draw their own districts have never been more sophisticated, and that the Supreme Court shows no inclination to stop them. I know that the Senate is the institutional expression of white, rural, minority rule, and that this is fine, because America is a republic not a democracy. I know what *autogolpe* means now. I suspect that American English is done being a net importer of authoritarian terms.

In June 2020, a reporter asked Justin Trudeau about

Donald Trump's threat to crush protestors with military force. Nothing sums up the Canadian response to all these developments better than Trudeau's famous twenty-one seconds of silence. Say what you will about him, but in that moment he spoke authentically for his people: our terror at the mere thought of antagonizing the big neighbour; our self-congratulatory sense that truly bad things happen elsewhere, leavened by a pro forma allowance that, of course, we aren't perfect ("It's time for us as Canadians to recognize that we too have our challenges").

Twenty months later, our capital was occupied, our crossings to America cut off, our Emergencies Act invoked for the first time. We too have our challenges.

It was commonly treated as a laugh line that one of the leaders of the Ottawa truck blockade, appearing in court, invoked his First Amendment rights. ("First Amendment?" asked the judge. "What's that?") But what a perfect illustration of the fact that the far-right movements in Canada and America are continuous with one another, that the forces that produced Trumpism in America are on the move here, too: the same political vocabulary, the same collective imagination, the same conspiracy theories, the same funding sources. The same difficulty, among the political class in both countries, in imagining a constructive response to those forces, beyond the sledgehammer of law enforcement.

What I heard in those twenty-one seconds of silence was the most eloquent expression possible of the great Canadian exemption, the idea that the forces upending

Introduction

democracies around the world somehow don't reach this far north. What I saw in the Ottawa blockade—our own, slow-motion January 6—was its convincing refutation. Our exemption has rarely seemed less secure.

If that is true, then asserting our difference—asserting it in a way that shapes our culture, our diplomacy, our domestic politics, our sense of ourselves—matters in this generation in a way that it has rarely mattered before. Because there *is* a difference, beginning with this, the basic fact that has yet to penetrate our politics: *our neighbour is an eroding democracy.* Canadian politics needs to start from that reality, because it is the political fact with the farthest-reaching consequences for Canadian life. Canada is not exempt from the polarization, the authoritarianism, and the conspiracizing that have put the future of American democracy into doubt. But Canada is different. If those forces are not so advanced here, it is not because Canada is congenitally behind the times. It is because our democracy can draw on a set of resources that are distinctively of this place. Canadian distinctiveness is not a vanity object: it is the essential safeguard of Canadian democracy.*

Reading reports of the first shots of the American Civil War, the Ontario Reform leader George Brown said simply: "We are glad we are not them." Our future depends on our ability to say something similar, and to

---

* Note that the words "Donald Trump" do not appear in this paragraph. The fixation on Trump's outrages and norm breaking is just a sophisticated form of denial, as if we could quarantine a vast historical process in the body of one elderly man who loves junk food.

13

mean it; to say it explicitly, not silently; to say it openly enough that it becomes an organizing principle of our national life, not simply a comforting excuse for our failures. Our future depends on our mental independence from America. The best tool we have for resisting democratic erosion is Canadian localism, especially as it applies to our eroding neighbour: in other words, steadily increasing Canadian separateness and distinctiveness from the United States.

In America's worst-case scenario, in which democratic erosion accelerates, Canadian localism can act as the buffer that keeps our democracy intact. But even in the better-case scenario, in which January 6 and all it represents ultimately shrink to a blip, Canadian localism still matters. We can't effectively protect our own institutions—from parliamentary government to a remarkable openness to immigration—without understanding what makes them our own. We can't aspire to anything meaningfully better until we are secure in our difference, until we stop seeing ourselves through American eyes.

In saying that, I do not mean to imply that Canada is some sort of privileged child of History, or that all of this is a matter of our purity and their contamination. If anything, for much of our history, things have been the other way around. When reformers in the Province of Canada first won their democracy in the 1840s, they were quite explicit about their project's American inspiration. After Confederation, it was America that sheltered Louis Riel and Canada that executed him. The RCMP swayed a federal election a decade before "but her emails" entered the

American political lexicon. What I have to offer is not some sort of transcendent truth about national characters, but rather a set of strategies adapted to the demands of this historical moment, taken in a broad sense—that is, the sense that does not expect the problem to be buried with Trump, the sense that does not expect the Canadian exemption to last in the absence of determined and creative action to lock it in place.

An eroding democracy is a threat to democracy in its neighbours. Think of the ways in which far-right and nativist forces collaborate across borders. Think of Tucker Carlson filming from Viktor Orbán's Hungary, or Steve Bannon's post-Trump career as a European fascist, or the cheers for Nigel Farage at a convention for American conservatives, or the pipeline of funding that connects Vladimir Putin and Marine Le Pen, or the 2023 reenactment of the Capitol riot, planned from Orlando and staged in Brasília. Globally, as measured by Freedom House, those forces have contributed to sixteen consecutive years of democratic erosion. Such forces bear on Canada in many ways, from alleged Chinese interference in the 2019 federal election to real estate prices in Vancouver or Toronto bid up by foreign oligarchs. But, by virtue of proximity and power, the most important conduits of democratic instability run due south.

Those conduits are symbolized by the roughly 44 percent of funding for the Ottawa blockade that originated in the United States, by its around-the-clock promotion on Fox News and other right-wing media, and by its celebration in the American far-right and antivax

Introduction

movements. In the words of a 2022 report issued by Canadian intelligence experts, including high-level advisors to both the Harper and Trudeau governments, "The United States is and will remain our closest ally, but it could also become a source of threat and instability." A little less cautiously, we might say that it already has. As one of the report's authors put it, "There are serious risks of democratic backsliding in the U.S., and at this point, that is not a theoretical risk. So all of that is a threat to our sovereignty, to our security, and in some cases, to our democratic institutions."

On their own, those facts are worrisome enough; in context, they are more so. The history of this hemisphere is a history of a hegemon willing and able to build up and pull down neighbouring governments—a history from which Canada has by no means been exempt. (Grant's *Lament for a Nation*, so pivotal in the history of Canadian nationalism, is among other things a protest against American interference in a Canadian election and encroachments on Canadian sovereignty.) It is hard to imagine a democratically eroded America being *more* friendly to Canadian democracy, a democracy that would begin to look like a standing rebuke.

More abstractly, America's power and prestige have always lent it a sort of political gravity. Powerful states, whatever their form of government, prompt envy and emulation. It seems as if they make the history the rest of us merely watch, as if they come from slightly in the future. They set the bounds of common sense within which the rest of us operate. Maybe an authoritarian

America would provoke only revulsion here—I'm sure it would in many of us. But authoritarianism wouldn't have a constituency if it didn't have its own glamour and appeal. Slowly and steadily, without any of us explicitly acknowledging its influence and many of us loudly disclaiming it, it would shape our sense of what is possible here—of what is permissible here. Resisting that process begins by looking the facts in the eye: the historical situation in which Canadians find themselves is fundamentally changed. Once, our connections to America were so many channels through which democratic ideas and practices entered our country; today, the situation is closer to the opposite. A free society cannot insulate itself from such influences, nor should it want to. But it can sharpen its critical capacity to assess and filter those influences as they arrive.

Our most potent weapon against antidemocratic ideas, whether they originate in Canada or elsewhere— and whether they go by the name of authoritarianism, illiberal democracy, right-wing populism, Trumpism, or something else—is our ability to stigmatize them as "alien," as eroding our difference along with our democracy. The fear of absorption—the creeping suspicion that we are not distinct, that we never were distinct, or that we are gradually losing our distinctiveness—has long been at the heart of Canadian nationalism. But as a motivating principle of our politics, it has also suffered from the two deficiencies I have pointed out: it is difficult to express or even care about when one is confronted with a knowledge of our colonizing past and present; and it is (especially in English Canada) the kind of vague and airy sentiment that can prompt occasional regret but not concerted action. But if we can begin to see how our search for distinctiveness is now bound to our fears for our democracy, we can also begin to see how those two problems may not be the final word.

First, tying our democracy to our difference helps us to understand one of the deep sources of our democratic resilience: the fact that we have always been a country of many nations, one that began with the Indigenous nations, grew to encompass francophone and anglophone Canada, and continues to be transformed by immigration. In the age of democratic decline, our multinational fact looks more like a saving grace than a stumbling block. Taking that fact as a starting point, we can develop a clearer idea of our difference—one that can replace once and for all the idea of colonized Canada.

Second, tying democracy to distinctiveness raises the stakes of the latter in a fundamental way. Our difference is not a luxury good, something for a rich and mostly contented people to worry about in the absence of more pressing concerns. On the contrary, it is our democratic immune system. And if that is the case, then the central challenge of Canadian politics at this moment is to develop and elaborate the idea of our difference; to discover, if we can, its deep roots in our history; and to give that idea an institutional and political expression.

Now, it is both cynical and easy to declare the politics you object to un-Canadian, or un-American, or generally un-us. Claims like that are the insects of the hour, which multiply and die out faster than we can count them, because they are essentially opportunistic. If many Canadians are skeptical of nationalism, it is not only because of the great and terrible things that have been done in its name, but because of the low and squalid things, as well. (It is also because, in a multinational country, it inevitably prompts the question, "Whose nationalism?") One way I've tried to acknowledge those worries is by sometimes using the term *localism*. *Nationalism* comes from the Latin for "birth," while *localism* comes from the Latin for "place." I think the latter conveys a sense of ourselves that is rooted in the land of which we are a part, and that does not lend itself to the troubling exclusions of an idea of belonging derived from natality: you cannot do anything to change your birth, but anyone can change, and be changed by, their place.

More to the point, any idea of Canadian difference—call it nationalism or localism or anything else—will prove unsustainable unless it is deeply rooted in some lasting facts of our centuries-long experience in this place, unless it reaches the level of myth. Myths are made by people—but people cannot make just any myth they want for just any purpose they choose. Myths are more difficult to use cynically (in, say, the way that Joseph McCarthy used "un-American"), because they have to be grounded so deeply in the history and culture of a place that they do not work smoothly for partisan purposes. To use them for such a purpose would be self-defeating, because your opponent's claim on them is just as strong as your own.

Canadians need to become better self-mythologizers. If we do not give ourselves a workable myth and a useable past, no one else will do it for us.

———

Saturated as we are by American media, and used to our position as a junior power on this continent, we often find it all too easy to see our difference through an American lens. What we see, and internalize, is a set of trivialities: milk in bags, beavers, some peculiar spellings. Even some potentially further-reaching facts, like universal health care, stand out in isolation, almost as accidents, maybe as objects that we are fearful of somehow misplacing. The prototypical American gesture towards Canada is a pat on the head. "A really nice apartment over a meth lab," in Robin Williams's famous line. America's Hat.

I don't want to read too deeply into that gesture, because it's the privilege of any empire not to take too deep an interest in its smaller, weaker neighbours.* But if there's any deeper reason at stake, I want to propose this one: America can't take both itself and Canada seriously, because taking Canada seriously is incompatible with its own myths.

Americans learn a hard and heroic myth, in which liberty from tyrants has to be purchased in blood, even

———

* It's the privilege of power of all sorts: for instance, a 1987 study found that wives "are capable of describing their husbands in great detail, whereas men can only describe their wives in very broad stereotypes valid for 'women in general.'"

at great moral cost. A few hours' drive north sits the counterexample. That counterexample has to be mentally disposed of: ignored if possible, trivialized if necessary. In case you'd respond that no one really thinks this way, consider how Americans continue to draw on this myth to understand their contemporary politics and to place their past failings in a redemptive light.

As I write this, PBS is airing a four-hour documentary on Benjamin Franklin and the American founding, directed by Ken Burns, who has defined the popular historical mainstream since the 1990s. When the documentary comes to Franklin's role in sealing America's constitutional compromises over slavery, Burns calls on a series of respected academic historians to provide the necessary exculpation. "The union is only possible if it includes the South," says one. But why was the union valuable in itself? "Unity and compromise was the only thing that could make this new nation move forward," says another. "Without it, it would be a failed journey. American democracy would not develop without it."

And there is the key claim: had America been unwilling to make its peace with slavery, it would have been reabsorbed into the empire of its day, and American democracy would have ended. Yet, if the Canadian experience is anything to go on, American democracy might have been delayed by roughly sixty years, and the abolition of slavery might have been advanced by roughly thirty. I'd consider that a fair trade. But the point is that it is impossible to even think in those terms, terms that are alive to historical contingency, as long as the story is conceived as messianic, apocalyptic: the end of our journey, the failure of democracy, the last great hope of earth, etc. Those otherworldly aims can justify, have justified, nearly any moral sacrifice.

It would be absurdly self-centred to claim that the picture Americans paint for themselves about their historical mission and their necessary compromises is in any way *about* Canada. Again, the privilege of empire: your picture is about no one but yourself.

Canada exists in that picture only as negative space. But at the same time, negative space, the part that is deliberately not filled in, defines the picture. Americans do not need to think about Canada to tell a meaningful story about themselves; they do need to leave Canada blank, or at least condescended to, which is much the same thing.

For our part, we do not need others to take us seriously. We do need to take ourselves seriously. In that regard, the problem is that the triviality we see reflected back at us is the product of someone else's needs, not our own. Much of our trouble in imagining ourselves as meaningfully separate serves political ends we never consented to and answers questions we ourselves never asked.

What I would like to do in this book is to help Canadians to think more deliberately about building our *structures of refusal*: deliberate, systematic choices about what to accept from our neighbour and what to reject, the choices through which we define and maintain our difference. We are what we refuse. In an age of democratic decline, Canada's democracy depends on refusal— serious, targeted, and creative.

This book is about our differences—that is, our refusals—and about our urgent need to think of them in a more explicit, organized way. Though there are many different ways into the problem, I want to start with the stories we tell ourselves about ourselves, and with the features of Canada's distinctive myth that offer powerful local resources against authoritarianism. Each of the first two chapters is about one such resource: first, Canada's myth of multiple foundings, and its refusal of the idea of a unitary people; second, Canada's myth of unheroic politics, and its refusal of revolution as a model of political change. Throughout, I'm using *myth* not in the sense of a falsehood, but of a collective story that orients us with respect to the past and the future. Myths are a kind of coordination point, and agreeing to treat a story as normative is no different in that regard from agreeing on a side of the road to drive on. The power is in the act of agreement. The more we agree that authoritarianism is structurally implausible here in Canada, the more that will in fact be the case.

I'm also going to look at the deep sources of American authoritarianism in history and myth. I'm not doing so because I believe that the United States is somehow fated to an undemocratic future, but rather because shock and bravado ("He can *do* that?!") are among the most powerful authoritarian weapons. Authoritarianism is less powerful when it is less shocking. One way to render it less shocking is to understand its roots in the past. And just as America's democratic instability did not materialize with Trump's 2015 escalator ride to his campaign announcement, it did not dissolve on Election Night 2022, either. Thinking in terms of history and myth can protect us from the minute-to-minute whipsawing between doom and salvation that is so destructive of strategic, deliberate political action.

We cannot simply will useful myths into being. But, with deliberation and care, we can exercise some collective power over the shapes they take. That collective power is the subject of the last two chapters, which discuss some concrete ways to make the story of an antiauthoritarian past and future plausible for a critical mass of Canadians. The third chapter is about the economic solidarity that makes democracy more than an empty slogan; the fourth is about democracy maintenance as a guiding principle of Canada's relations with the world.

———

That will do by way of summary—but on reflection I find that it is missing the truth of feeling.

Let me try again: Somewhere along the way, my country of birth went wrong. I have some advice, about where and why that happened, to give to my country of choice.

I spoke earlier about the narcissism of small differences. Let me speak now about the desperation of small differences. At times it seems as if the visible signs of our difference are so small and so slight that I'm a fool to hang so much on them. And then the light shifts, and they become the evidence of things unseen: the long *o* in *process* and *tomorrow* and *sorry*; "washrooms"; "lineups"; waiting for the light to change at the crosswalk, without a car in sight; the late onset of summer, so joyful that it hurts. *Things will be different here.* When the news from home is particularly bad, I'm embarrassed that things so trivial should be so consoling, ashamed by the intensity with which I want to believe that things will be different here, by the fear that they will not be.

I've been singing my daughters the ABC song at bedtime their whole lives. I changed it when we moved here: "W, X, Y, and zed." *Things will be different here.* My youngest daughter is just a few months older than this book. My middle daughter has been here since she was two months old; she came in her sleep, facing backwards in a bucket car seat in a van trailing the U-Haul, and that version is the only one she knows. But my oldest daughter still remembers when I sang it to her in our tiny apartment in the States, and she knows something about the difficulty of leaving; and whenever I try to change the last letter, she reacts with outrage that anyone would violate the sanctity of the alphabet. Before I can end, she claps her hand over my mouth: "Zee, man. It's *zee.*"

Part I
MYTH

Chapter 1

FOUNDINGS

ON JANUARY 6, 2021, DONALD Trump addressed the crowd that had gathered in Washington, DC, to fight for its president and his claim on power: "You're the real people. You're the people who built this nation. You're not the people who tore down our nation." Of course those words launched a riot. How much bloodshed has been sanctioned by that magic thought, the people, the *real* people? Imagine that those words were true: that some impostor had taken away the power that was yours by right. What kind of coward would you be if you *didn't* fight back?

The idea that does the violent work here—that turns the democratic commonplace of popular rule into a call to insurrection—is the idea of the *real* people. The real people are entitled to govern by virtue of their reality. Their reality is defined in opposition to some other group: in this case, "the people who tore down our nation." Sorting one group from the other is not a matter of numbers: you don't identify a genuine hundred-dollar bill in a stack of counterfeits by counting, but by looking for the qualities that mark it as authentic. And that kind of qualitative sorting, not the mechanical counting of votes, becomes the supposed basis of democracy: any election the real people lose is stolen, by definition. Call this the "Real People Principle."

The Real People Principle is the ideological heart of America's democratic instability, and Trump's invocation of it put him in a long authoritarian tradition. The Real People Principle is a threat to majority rule in any diverse democracy, Canada included. The difference—and a major reason for democracy's comparatively stronger position north of the border—is that the idea of the Real People is less plausible in Canada. There is no single Canadian people, real or otherwise. There never has been. For the most part, we have come to understand ourselves as a country of multiplicities and of multiple foundings. Today, our multiplicity is the key to our democratic resilience. And we should see efforts to erase that multiplicity as the dangers they are.

———

Think of "the people" as an atomic nucleus, a store of immense and explosive energy, capable of powering cities or flattening them—and, just as important, an object imperceptible to the naked eye. In a democracy like Canada, we say that "the people rule," but already that statement is a fiction. It makes sense only if you leave out children, nonvoting residents, citizens who don't bother to vote, and so on; and again, only if you leave out the citizens who are outvoted in any given election; and again, only if you accept the questionable premise that the officials who govern are meaningfully controlled by the people who vote. It is an act of imagination to say that the people rule—or rather, it is half a dozen acts of imagination, all happening simultaneously.

And that's fine! Our lives are structured by all kinds of shared imaginings—money, for instance, or the days of the week—that are no less valid or important for all that they are insubstantial. But this means that there will *always* be an irreducible gap between the real, flesh-and-blood people who go about their lives in a certain place and the imagined entity of "the people" that is supposed to rule it: the people in the supermarket, and "the people" as exalted sovereign. Deciding how to align these two categories is always a political struggle. In many ways, it is *the* political struggle.

In fact, one way of understanding the modern history of democracy is as a story of flesh-and-blood people demanding entry, often violently, into the category of the people who rule. In prerevolutionary France, six months before the storming of the Bastille, Abbé Sieyès famously spoke on behalf of the Third Estate, the great mass of people who were neither nobles nor clergy, and who were virtually shut out from political power on that account:

What is the Third Estate? Everything.

What has it been so far in the political order? Nothing.

What does it want to be? Something.

Those words express a foundational democratic idea: a world in which the "everything" of the flesh-and-blood people is denied its fair share in political rule is no longer tolerable. How much constitutes a fair share? An amount between "nothing" and "everything." Think of the subsequent centuries of democratic politics as a struggle to define that amount. And think of how they were shaped by efforts to make the construction of "the people" look as natural and inevitable as possible. In literal terms, the Third Estate was not "everything"; still less were Sieyès and those others who claimed to speak on its behalf. But hedged and qualified statements rarely make revolutions.

This basic operation—some proportion of the people is equal to "the people"—has never left us. The eighteenth-century revolutionaries established both the sovereignty of "the people" (in theory) and the sovereignty of propertied white men (in fact). In the generations since, when the tension between the theory and the fact grew unbearable, revolutionary successors set out to amend their work.

In his monumental history *Black Reconstruction*, W. E. B. Du Bois gives us a portrait of one of those revolutionaries at the moment he ran up against the brick wall of political reaction. The year is 1866. The American Civil War is over, and slavery has just been abolished by constitutional amendment. Now Frederick Douglass and a delegation of Black leaders are at the White House to demand action on voting rights from Andrew Johnson, a Tennessee populist elevated to the presidency by Abraham Lincoln's assassination.

President Johnson is not convinced. "Was it proper to put on a people, without their consent, Negro suffrage?" he asked Douglass. "Do you deny that first great principle of the right of the people to govern themselves?" A member of the delegation asked whether that principle applied in South Carolina, where the majority of the people were Black. The narrative goes on:

> He could not touch the question as to whether it was right to prevent a majority in South Carolina from ruling because, to his mind, no number of Negroes could outweigh the will of whites. . . . "It is a fundamental tenet of my creed that the will of the people must be obeyed. Is there anything wrong or unfair in that?"
>
> Douglass smiled, still thinking of South Carolina: "A great deal that is wrong, Mr. President, with all respect."

Soon after, the meeting ends at an impasse.

> Douglass, turning to leave, said: "The President sends us to the people and we go to the people."
>
> "Yes, sir," answered the President, "I have great faith in the people."

In their last exchange, Douglass and Johnson use the same term—"the people"—to mean diametrically opposed things. It would be high comedy if it were not the prelude to a century of terrorism. Four years later, universal male suffrage entered the Constitution—where it sat inert, a mere paper right, for most of the next century. Douglass would live to see the argument resolved, by bloodshed, in Johnson's favour. At that moment in history, one suspects, the argument could not have been ended one way or the other by any other means. When it came to the key point of contention, Douglass and Johnson, and the political forces they represented, simply did not speak the same language. I read the narrative of their meeting and think of the story of the fish who doesn't know what water is: the inherent whiteness of "the people" is the water in which Johnson has swum his whole life, and no amount of prodding can even bring him to notice it, let alone question it.

If you want to understand where American democracy stands at this moment, try understanding Andrew Johnson. Try understanding how denying the vote to a majority of the people can be a vindication of "the people"—how voting rights can be imposed on a people "without their consent"—how self-government can destroy "the right of the people to govern themselves." You might call those turns of language Orwellian, but Orwell himself told us that the truly frightening thing about such ideas is the complete sincerity with which they are held. "He is not pretending," he wrote of a man who held such inconceivable ideas, "he is not a hypocrite, he believes every word he says." I doubt there is much of a future in America for an authoritarian movement that sees itself as authoritarian. There is still a promising future, and a deep-rooted past, for an authoritarian movement that sees itself as a crusade for democracy.

Behind the statewide "audits" of the 2020 election; behind the paranoia over compromised voting machines, "harvested" ballots, and fraudulent vote-by-mail; behind the emerging body of legal theory that would empower state legislatures to override voters and choose the president themselves; behind the siege of the Capitol, and the machinations to overturn future elections at the hands of state officials and judges, not rioters and insurrectionists, there is a consistent and coherent set of beliefs about who "the people" are and who they are not. President Trump has said as much, explicitly. His movement said so just a little less explicitly when it identified such cities as Atlanta, Detroit, Philadelphia, and Milwaukee as the heartland of electoral fraud. As the *New York Times* columnist Jamelle Bouie points out, Atlanta and Detroit are majority Black, while Philadelphia and Milwaukee are home to their states' highest concentrations of Black voters. "The larger implication is clear enough: a majority made up of liberals and nonwhites isn't a real majority. And the solution is clear, too: to write those people out of the polity, to use every available tool to weaken their influence on American politics."

That election is over, of course. And so is the 2022 midterm election, in which Democrats—buoyed by their defense of abortion rights and by the extremism of their opponents—dramatically outperformed expectations and evicted from office a number of the right's most prominent election denialists. Given those hopeful results, it can seem an act of paranoia in its own right to harp on cases in which the worst was averted. In fact, many on the American left have plausibly argued that liberals' fixation on January 6 and the authoritarian threat is less about the genuine state of democracy than about liberals' need to dramatize themselves as democracy's heroic defenders, to imagine themselves as the Resistance even when they are in power.* I'm sympathetic to that argument. But I'm not fully convinced by it, because the idea of the stolen election and the Real People from whom it was allegedly stolen is not about an election at all. Rather, it is the justification for an active and ongoing project of democratic erosion—a project that is absolutely capable of surviving electoral setbacks.

That is why the continuity between Andrew Johnson and Donald Trump—between the white supremacy of the nineteenth century and the authoritarianism of the twenty-first—strikes me as such a helpful framework for understanding where we find ourselves. I am as prone as anyone to imagine American politics as the kind of heroic narrative that generations of mass culture have trained us to see everywhere: a near-death experience for

---

* As an aside, the *Star Wars* sequel trilogy, which spanned the late Obama years and Trump's term in office, is a perfect pop culture expression of the permanent-Resistance attitude. While our heroes begin the trilogy as the galactic government, the filmmakers almost immediately demote them back to the familiar role of scrappy rebels, seemingly incapable of imagining what they would do with actual power.

democracy in 2020, followed by the triumph of the good guys and the return to normal in 2022. But *normal*, in America, is frightening enough.

Normal includes permanent voter suppression and enforced one-party rule on the state level. In Georgia, Republican lawmakers created hours-long voting lines by eliminating polling places in nonwhite neighbourhoods — and then made it illegal to hand out water to the voters they forced to wait.[*] In Florida, an overwhelming majority of voters (64 percent) approved a 2018 referendum restoring voting rights to ex-felons. Florida's Republican legislature and Republican governor, Ron DeSantis, moved immediately to nullify the result by imposing poll taxes on the new voters, in an explicit return to segregationist tradition. In 2022, DeSantis created a state elections police force. That summer, it sent the public a message: a series of highly publicized arrests of Florida citizens who had committed "voter fraud" under the incorrect belief that they had been legally reenfranchised. Three months later, DeSantis was reelected in a nineteen-point landslide, which would be a very impressive margin in a democracy. Among regimes in which state security forces intimidate opponents out of voting, it is roughly par for the course.

In states like Wisconsin, Republican legislators have undertaken rigorous, data-driven redistricting processes,

---

[*] The state's rationale is that providing voters with food, or even water, might constitute bribery. Incidentally, a 2016 Supreme Court decision made it drastically more difficult to convict elected officials for accepting bribes in exchange for political favours.

effectively breaking the link between election results and political control. There, gerrymandering essentially guarantees Republicans a state legislative majority, even with a minority of votes—as in 2018, when they won fewer State Assembly votes than Democrats and still awarded themselves almost two-thirds of the seats. Voters who want to change party control of the legislature have been rendered powerless to do so—by people calling themselves their representatives. Political scientists have concluded that gerrymandering is nearly as extreme in fourteen other states—and that incumbents in those states have proven as skilled at freeing themselves from their voters as their counterparts in such "closed democracies" as Albania, Cambodia, Ethiopia, and Venezuela. In this context, the idea of state legislators choosing presidential electors themselves is more than a fringe legal theory or a radical departure from the norm: it is a logical extension of the deep voter-proofing that is already in place.

By gutting the Voting Rights Act in 2013, and by shielding partisan gerrymandering from federal oversight in 2019, the Supreme Court has extended its protection to these state-level manipulations. In Ohio, Alabama, Louisiana, and Georgia, Republicans have openly defied lower court rulings that their congressional district maps were unconstitutionally rigged along racial or partisan lines. The Supreme Court condoned partisan gerrymandering in Florida as well. In 2022, these maps provided the margin for Republican control of the US House of Representatives.

Normal includes political institutions that are fundamentally hostile to the idea of equal political power.

In the words of Steven Levitsky, a political scientist and coauthor of *How Democracies Die*, the United States is "far and away the most counter-majoritarian democracy in the world." The 2020 election left a US Senate evenly divided between Republicans and Democrats—in which the Democratic half represented some 41.5 million more Americans. In 2017, 2018, and 2020, a president elected by a minority of Americans nominated three Supreme Court justices, who were confirmed by senators representing a minority of Americans, and who now enjoy lifetime, unaccountable power to strike down laws that any future majority might care to pass. The Senate filibuster gives veto power to senators representing as little as 10 percent of the national population.

The allotment of the same number of senators to each state is the only element of the US Constitution that is explicitly impossible to amend. So as Americans continue to migrate to more populous states, their political power— not very equal to begin with—will grow more and more diluted. By 2040, it is projected that 70 percent of Americans will be represented by thirty senators—which is to say that they will be politically impotent on the federal level. We can also expect the increasingly explicit defense of this power shift as an affirmative good, as the return of power to rural, white America, to the Real People.

And *normal* includes the perennial possibility of political violence. A minority that owes its power to judicial fiat and the manipulation of the rules is not likely to feel especially secure in its power. It will continue to understand itself as encircled, embattled, outnumbered.

It will increasingly resemble other ruling minorities that so memorably combined a sense of entitlement and a sense of siege: the southern planters, the Afrikaners of the apartheid era, the Anglo-Irish Ascendancy.

Under these conditions, political violence will be more than the sporadic explosions of angry young men. It will be a principle of rule. It will express itself in the storied language of liberty, tyranny, and constitutional order. It will issue regular threats of prison rape or reprisals from "Second Amendment people," in Trump's words, or "trial by combat," in Rudy Giuliani's. Its enemies will be defined as "groomers," child molesters, sexual deviants—simply because, in American politics circa 2023, these are the words one uses to mark a political enemy as worthy of death.

Some of this violence will be spectacular and organized, as on January 6; more of it will be virtually invisible, except to the school board member driven into hiding, the public health official cornered in a parking lot after a town meeting, the election worker with death threats in her inbox. "You will all be executed." "Wire around their limbs and tied & dragged by a car." "I KNOW WHERE YOU SLEEP, I SEE YOU SLEEPING."

What Ida B. Wells observed about the violence of lynch law in the twentieth century will be equally true of authoritarian violence in the twenty-first: "It is not the creature of an hour, the sudden outburst of uncontrolled fury, or the unspeakable brutality of an insane mob. It represents the cool, calculating deliberation of intelligent people." It is, for lack of a better term, *normal*.

It is unambiguously hopeful that American voters rejected so many denialists, conspiracists, and authoritarians in 2022. But I am not convinced that those results offer a way out of the essential dilemma; a two-party democracy in which one party rejects democracy is always under a stay of execution. For more than a decade, Democratic leaders have been predicting that "the fever may break" (in President Obama's words) after a sufficiently convincing Republican loss. But in a polarized and closely divided country, in which Republicans are well insulated from public opinion, and in which a swing of a relative handful of votes in the right places can deliver unopposed power, the old guidelines—including "moderate in response to a loss"—no longer apply.

A week before the 2022 election, the Republican candidate for governor of Wisconsin told his supporters that "Republicans will never lose another election in Wisconsin after I'm elected." He lost by just over three percentage points. Part of me wants to celebrate that result as a tidy story of political crime and electoral punishment. Part of me remembers the words the IRA made famous after a failed assassination attempt: "We only have to be lucky once. You will have to be lucky always."

As for the Democratic leadership, its moral indignation has been pitch-perfect. In recent years, President Biden has given us a "battle for the soul of this nation," "moments so stark that they divide all that came before them from everything that followed," and even Republican "semi-fascism." And I can't quibble with the electoral results. But ultimately, what Biden and his party have had to offer is increasingly apocalyptic rhetoric (I fully expect him to drop the "semi-" by 2024) in the service of resolutely ordinary appeals: vote, donate, like, subscribe.

That gap between words and action may be enough for short-term success, but it barely responds to the long-term problem, in which "semi-fascists" govern nearly half the states and make a plausible bid for national power every two years. I understand that presidents can't conjure votes from thin air, and that the odds of action to weaken state-level voter suppression or mitigate the undemocratic Constitution were always remote in the short term. But if America were really in danger of falling to fascism, wouldn't Biden's appeal to the public be fundamentally different from the call to elect Democrats to office that he has been making every two years since 1972? Wouldn't this be a time for extraordinarily creative action? That no such action is forthcoming—not a public confrontation with the Supreme Court, not a plan to expand the court or check its power through legislation, not a federal intervention to break up one-party cartels at the state level, not a sustained push for the admission of new states, not the expulsion of insurrectionists from Congress—suggests that much of the starkness-of-this-moment talk is what wrestling fans call *kayfabe*. The absence of this creativity marks the difference between a merely successful presidency and a truly realigning one.

In all of this, Biden represents a powerful strand of American liberalism that tends to see regular backlashes against democracy—more specifically, regular white backlashes against multiracial democracy—as part of the natural order of things, as predictable and unchangeable as the tides. But one of the most compelling spokesmen for this theory of history has been his Democratic predecessor. Here is how President Obama summed it up in a 2021 interview:

> That's been the history of America, right? There is abolition, and the Civil War, and then there's backlash, and the rise of the KKK, and then Reconstruction ends, and Jim Crow arises, and then you have a civil rights movement, a modern civil rights movement, and desegregation. And that in turn leads to pushback and ultimately Nixon's Southern strategy. What I take comfort from is that in the traditional two steps forward, one step back, as long as you're getting the two steps, then the one step back, you know, is the price of doing business.

"Two steps forward, one step back" may be Obama's single favourite metaphor, one that he used on some two dozen occasions as president. And no wonder—it is a compelling piece of liberal theodicy. It is an effort to explain why suffering is meaningful and ultimately justified, why bad things happen to good people. And like all theodicy, it is an appeal to faith. The math of two parts progress to one part regress simply has to work—and has to keep working *indefinitely*—for all that pain to make sense. Even if it does (and, to be fair, Obama acknowledged in the same interview that there are sometimes "three steps back"), it is entirely possible for whole human lives to be contained in the parenthesis of backlash—for generations to be born and to die within the step back. I can't take much consolation from the idea that History has a plan for any of our suffering, that any amount of evil we endure now pays the toll for distant others to live better lives, later. But if it does, then periods of relative unfreedom are both inevitable and inconsequential—inconsequential, at least, in the long view, in which they will ultimately be redeemed.

This is as mainstream a progressive belief as I can think of: in a sense, it defines what it means to be "progressive." But it is difficult to reconcile with a belief in a crisis of democracy. The two beliefs may be logically consistent—it is certainly possible to have a localized crisis within a generalized story of uplift—but they are not emotionally consistent. When senior Democrats express both beliefs at the same time, as they regularly do, I wonder: Can you truly experience a crisis as a crisis if you also define it as predictable, temporary, and the down payment on a better world? How much urgency can you really summon if your sense of history—if your sense of yourself as a historical actor—derives from a story in which everything will continue to turn out okay?

Worse, "two steps forward, one step back" is a model that treats liberal failure as expected and excused even as it is happening. There is no alternative to a world in which the forces of reaction return to power every generation or so, brandishing the club of the Real People. Failure has already been preexplained and preaccounted for. Disappointing as these regular periods of tribulation may be, they are the necessary price of redoubled liberal success.

Though phrased as a sober counsel of realism—backlash and reaction are inevitable—the progressive idea of history is in fact deeply utopian. Every success has to be bigger than the last success, every failure has to be more piddling than the last failure, or the moral calculus falls apart. One day, the round hole will be so worn down that the square peg will fit snugly.

And maybe, one day, it will. But—writing as I am from within one of those periodic and recurrent moments of failure—I wonder about the interchangeability of Andrew Johnson and Donald Trump, about the sheer tenacity of the Real People Principle as a force in American politics, about its seemingly permanent availability as *the* reactionary move.

Writing as I am from Canada, I wonder whether there isn't another way of approaching the problem. If American politics is a constant struggle over who constitutes "the people," Canadian politics tends to deny that there is such a thing as "the people" at all. In a country that understands itself as multinational, the Real People Principle—the idea of assigning political power on the basis of some qualitative test of authentic membership—has less power to endanger democracy.

Of course, undemocratic populism is a force in Canadian life: to take a recent example, the tactical sophistication, deep funding networks, and ex-military leadership of the Ottawa blockade made it look less like an act of civil disobedience than an unrepresentative minority's grasp at political rule. The RCMP fields so many violent threats against politicians that, in 2022, it ran short of officers to staff security details—even for the prime minister. At the same time, Canada's leading extremists—Maxime Bernier, Derek Sloan, Faith Goldy, or Ezra Levant, for instance—would all be met with open arms in the current Republican Party. Even in the mainstream of Canadian conservatism, Stephen Harper closed out the 2015 election by distinguishing "old-stock Canadians" from the rest of us.

Yet for the most part, a sharp contrast continues to hold: on the one hand, a broad Canadian consensus on the maintenance of democracy amidst demographic change; on the other hand, an America in which democracy itself is just one more polarizing issue. So far, there is no Canadian equivalent of American election denialism, permanently unrepresentative institutions, and mainstreaming of political violence. That contrast is all the more surprising given that the historical enormities that might explain the difference—Indigenous genocide, the presence of slavery, racialized immigration restriction—are as Canadian as they are American.

Still, there is at least one Canadian historical process that does not have its American counterpart, and I think we can find in that process the roots of whatever democratic resilience Canada might have. That process is the ongoing rejection of a single Canadian people. In one sense, there has never been such a people. In another sense, the growing place that that absence has in

Canadians' self-understanding is a newer development. It was, in fact, the most important development in Canada's recent history: a change that amounted to a refounding of Canada.

———

Both Canada and America passed through parallel attempts at refoundings in the middle of the last century. Canada's refounding undermined the idea of a single people; America's attempted to open membership in "the people" to all Americans. Canada's refounding was largely successful; America's—in many ways the more difficult and more heroic project—was bitterly contested and remains incomplete.

A founding is a fundamental change in a political community—a change in its institutions, its myths, its sense of history. It remakes the community as something new. But communities cannot burst into existence from nowhere: all foundings are refoundings, and vice versa.

A founding stretches forwards and backwards in time. It does not simply change where the community is going. It rewrites the story of the past, promoting some events, people, and principles to a new significance, effacing others from public memory. Foundings set up new memorials and tear down old ones, sometimes figuratively and sometimes quite literally. When a founding is successful—and by successful, I simply mean the amoral question of whether it "takes"—it is retrospective. In 1870, France overthrew its emperor and created the Third Republic. It also created, retrospectively, the First Republic of 1792 and the Second Republic of 1848—turning what could have been aberrations, dead ends, into honoured predecessors. In this century, Russia has been refounded as something like a fascist state. One measure of the thoroughness of this change is the way in which the public memory of the Soviet Union has been limited, to the exclusion of nearly everything else, to its victory in the Great Patriotic War (which we call World War II). A successful founding changes the past.

A moment ago, I wrote something straightforward about the Canadian past: that there has never been a single Canadian people. I believe that that is a true statement— but it is also a statement from *within* the world of historical memory created by Canada's refounding. For much of Canadian history, it would have been possible to tell an entirely different story, a story situated within a different world of memory. That was the world of *Wacousta*, of white settlers confronting an unforgiving wilderness, of First Nations doomed to assimilate or vanish. It was the world of Lord Durham's report on the Canadas, in which French Canadians figure as a community "destitute of all that can invigorate and elevate a people . . . a people with no history, and no literature," in which their gradual extinction and the achievement of responsible government are touted as equally progressive goals. It was the world in which the French language was presumed to be a quaint and dying holdover of a defeated people, the world in which the state sent guns rather than gifts to the Red River and Batoche, the world in which "half-breed" was a census category. It was the world in which the Canadian state wrote treaties not as compacts between sovereign equals, but as documents of surrender, in which the Indigenous signatories "do hereby cede, release, surrender and yield up to the Government of Canada for her Majesty the Queen and Her successors forever, all their rights, titles and privileges whatsoever." It was the world in which immigration from Asia, in the words of John A. Macdonald, was "abhorrent to the Aryan race and Aryan principles." It was the world of the residential schools.

From this perspective (the dominant perspective for a good deal of our history), there was a single, real Canadian people: white, Protestant, and anglophone, destined to absorb, exclude, or extinguish all else in its path. The arrow of history pointed towards homogeneity. That view was hardly unique to Canada; it was the consensus of the white world and the negation of multiracial democracy. Had it continued to be a dominant view in Canada—perhaps with the more bigoted edges sanded down, but still essentially intact—there is every reason to believe that we would now be living through a crisis of democracy as acute as the American crisis.

Something happened to prevent it. What was it? In the very long view, it was the multiple foundings of distinct political societies—the Indigenous nations and the societies of French and English Canada—with their incommensurable histories and traditions, none of which proved capable of absorbing the others, and all of which proved resistant to absorption. In the more immediate view, it was the more-or-less mutual recognition of these foundings as equally valid, a recognition brought about by Indigenous and French Canadian struggles for self-determination, and by the Anglo Canadian retreat from assimilationist aims. This process of mutual recognition constitutes Canada's modern refounding. The result is a country without a single, sovereign people.

The idea of Canada as a multinational democracy invites a number of misconceptions, which are especially sticky because of the way they flatter Canadian vanity. One is that Canada's founding "pillars" have succeeded in accommodating one another as a result of their superlative virtue, their skill in compromise and mutual understanding. No doubt those qualities had a role to play—but much more important, as the historian Peter H. Russell has pointed out, is Canada's history of "incomplete conquests." The relevant virtues were not so much kindness and tolerance as stubbornness, on the one hand, and a capacity for coming to terms with failure, on the other. Nor was Canada's twentieth-century refounding a cuddly and considerate process. Like all political foundings, it was a trial by fire. Its landmarks include the uprising against the 1969 White Paper and the October Crisis; its outcomes nearly included the end of the federation; its relevant political emotions begin with acrimony and rage, not sympathy and comity. Those come later, if at all.

Another misconception is that the mutual recognition of Canada's founding pillars does *positive* political work—that is, that it meaningfully solves anyone's problems. It clearly does not—as demonstrated, for example, by the three dozen First Nations reserves with boil-water advisories as of this writing. All the political work that our mutual recognition has done is *negative*. That is, it weakens the ability of any one group to speak on behalf of all Canadians. Canada's refounding was essentially successful because it ended in some degree of consensus—agreement on the proposition that its pillars are distinct political societies with their own powers and rights. Yet as important as that consensus is, it is also a minimal consensus. It left the details of those powers and rights the subject of intense conflict. It did not abolish racism or the legacies of colonialism. It did not stop a third of Canadians from telling a national pollster in 2022 that white people in Canada face more discrimination than visible minorities. And it certainly did not establish substantive equality or justice among the Canadian peoples.

Then what *did* it establish? The twentieth-century refounding was the period when Canada became a country without a Real People. Its pivotal moments include the revolt against the White Paper and the Canadian state's disavowal of the policy of Indigenous assimilation. The Quiet Revolution, the development of Québécois nationalism, and the assertion of French-language rights that culminated in Bill 101. The adoption of official multiculturalism and bilingualism. The *Calder* decision, the recognition in principle of aboriginal title, and the beginnings of a modern treaty process. The beginnings of mass immigration from outside Europe and the remaking of

Canada's ethnic composition. On one end of this tremendously fertile period, Canada adopted a new flag, and on the other, a new constitution, incorporating aboriginal and treaty rights. Surely both are powerful markers of a new founding, and they suggest the years 1965 and 1982 as rough chronological bookends.

What these disparate and contentious moments have in common is the emptying out of the Real People. It was a result achieved by a huge diversity of political actors and social movements, often working at cross-purposes, but pushing, consciously or not, towards a common goal. It was through this messy and confusing and often infuriating process of refounding, carried out in fits and starts over roughly two decades, that Canadians came to reject the idea of a single, sovereign people.* Indeed, Canadians came to find—through the reassessment of history involved in all successful refoundings—that such a people had never been there at all.

All these historical developments are familiar to Canadians. In bringing them together under the idea of a modern refounding, I am only restating the obvious.† But

---

* Limiting the period of refounding to approximately two decades represents, of course, an arbitrary cutoff. But if we were to trace the same historical processes into the 1990s, we could include the failure of the second Quebec independence referendum, which ensured that the Québécois would continue as a nation within Canada for the foreseeable future, and the *Delgamuukw* decision, which incorporated Indigenous oral history into Canadian law.

† The idea of a twentieth-century refounding is also debatable. There is a plausible case for situating the crucial period much further in the past, in Baldwin and LaFontaine's early binational collaboration in the united Prov-

myths are made out of the obvious; no other material is suitable. Votes and legislation and court decisions happen every year. What does not happen every year—what may not happen in a lifetime—is an accretion of prosaic political events capable of changing the story we tell ourselves about ourselves, a narrative whole that becomes greater than the sum of its parts. Given the capacity of the Real People Principle to subvert democracy, it matters profoundly that we can tell ourselves a story that is more than a list of dates on a blackboard, a story about how the power of the Real People was pushed to the margins of Canadian political life. Like all broad historical narratives, it admits counterexamples and charges of oversimplification—but even if such a thing as scientific accuracy were possible in history, myths do not aspire to that goal. Their goal is plausibility, and the test of plausibility is whether they are persuasive enough to motivate political action.

Canadian political life is organized around an absence, the empty space where the Real People used to be. But how do we observe the effects of an absence?

For one, think of the continued failure of anti-immigration to emerge as a serious force in Canadian politics, a fact that sets Canada apart from nearly all other

<hr>

ince of Canada in the 1840s. But it seems to me that the Baldwin-LaFontaine partnership, as crucial as it was as a precedent for Canada's multinational future, does not quite rise to the level of the modern refounding. First, it was only *bi*national: it did not imagine a future for Indigenous nationhood in Canada. Second, it did not prevent the resurgence of Anglo Canadian assimilationist policies (in Manitoba, for instance) after Confederation. In other words, I would consider it an incomplete or attempted refounding, rather than a founding that "took."

rich democracies. Brian Mulroney, the former Conservative prime minister, calls for Canada to triple its population by the end of the century, and no one blinks. The
Trudeau government announces plans for half a million
new immigrants per year, and no one coughs. Pierre Poilievre launches a right-populist bid for leadership of the
Conservative Party, and while we would expect a similarly situated politician in any other rich democracy to
put immigration at the centre of his campaign, it is virtually absent. Fox News terrifies American retirees with
footage of migrant "caravans," Australia detains migrants
on island prisons, billboard vans bearing the message GO
HOME OR FACE ARREST trawl through immigrant neighbourhoods in Britain, and Canadian anti-immigration
continues to be the dog that didn't bark.

As with the mutual recognition of the founding
peoples, we have many ways to account for Canada's
broad immigration consensus without resorting to hand-
waving about Canadian kindness. Explanations are not
hard to come by: Canada's only land border is with a
wealthier country; Canada's "points-based" immigration system is in fact more selective than America's; the
settlement patterns of new Canadians, especially in the
Greater Toronto Area, make them politically pivotal and
therefore foolish targets for demonization. But even so,
those straightforward explanations seem to explain too
little. Britain and Australia show how political cultures
of hostility to immigrants do not require land borders
at all. America shows how immigrants' political power
is just as likely to galvanize nativist backlash. The fact

that new Canadians are a powerful voting bloc does not explain how they emerged as a voting bloc in the first place—how, for instance, Canada maintains the highest naturalization rate in the world.

For a full account of the Canadian immigration consensus, we need to understand why anti-immigrant ideas have so little plausibility here in the first place. Anti-immigrant ideas generally rest on a foundational belief, the existence of a Real People that immigrants supposedly displace. So it matters profoundly that that belief holds so little purchase in modern Canadian politics. As a result of the Canadian refounding, the Real People is *already* displaced. A word like *diversity* captures something of this reality, but only superficially. Many countries are diverse; fewer owe their modern existence to a political struggle against homogeneity.

Again, the outcome of that political struggle extends both forwards and backwards in time. Extending forwards, it means that it will likely take more than an opportunistic politician or party to unsettle the Canadian consensus on immigration. That's no reason for complacency: refoundings would be impossible if political consensus never broke down. But it does suggest that threats to the immigration consensus, such as that posed by the Coalition Avenir Québec (CAQ), are likely to be filtered through Canada's multinationalism in a distinctive way (a point I'll return to at the end of this chapter). Extending backwards, the struggle reshapes Canadians' sense of where the past had been heading: history's arrow no longer points towards homogeneity.

Now the past reveals something else. In the words of John Ralston Saul—whose work offers a profound account of Canada's essentially Indigenous character—it shows us "a non-racial idea of civilization, and non-linear, even non-rational. It is based on the idea of an inclusive circle that expands and gradually adapts as new people join us. This is not a Western or European concept. It comes straight from Aboriginal culture." I would amend this only to point out that, like the idea that there has never been a single Canadian people, this is a view from inside the refounding. Perhaps our recent experience of immigration derives from "our unbroken past here." But the past is always broken. And our memory is always selective.

Refoundings build up and tear down. We can observe the absence of the Real People in the growth of the immigration consensus—but we can also observe it in the outbreak of grief and rage over the discovery of the mass graves at the residential schools in Kamloops, Marieval, Brandon, and Cranbrook, to name just a few. As much as those graves came as a dark revelation, I'm struck by the degree to which they were no revelation at all. They confirmed a truth already widely known—to the victims, of course, the families to which the students never returned, but known as well to the thousands who staffed those schools over the generations, to the churches that operated them, to the government officials who funded them. The schools were less a conspiracy of silence than a conspiracy of indifference. What sort of psychological armor would one have needed to dig those graves, again and again, to lower those small bodies into the ground? The armor of ideology, of unstoppable historical purpose: a shield from the knowledge of good and evil.

We're quite familiar with the process of ideological indifference-making, of political omelets and broken human eggs, when it happens elsewhere. It is the template with which we try to make sense of the Inquisition, the Gulag, the Jakarta Method. For decades, it was eminently possible to know the full details of the Stalinist show trials and to keep faith with communism. To denounce the trials, explained a prominent leftist priest in France, "is to play the imperialists' game." *Decades* of this.

And then, one day, the armor cracked. It cracked for different men and women on different days—but the great day of disillusionment, in the judgment of the historian Tony Judt, was August 21, 1968, the day that Soviet tanks rolled into Czechoslovakia to crush the Prague Spring: "The illusion that Communism was reformable . . . was crushed under the tanks on August 21st 1968 and it never recovered." Across Europe, intelligent men and women could content themselves with atrocities in the belief that they were the mortar of a better world. Only when that belief was finally exhausted—when it was indisputably clear that there was no better world in the offing, just bayonets and tank treads—could they look reality in the face.

We're quite familiar with this process when it happens elsewhere; it has happened here, too. White Canadians' self-recrimination over the residential schools, the cancelled Canada Day celebrations, the flags at half-mast for more than a year: these were not reactions to an essentially new set of facts. They were reactions to facts confronted, like the tanks in Prague, in a state of ideological nakedness. In our case, that ideology was assimilation and homogeneity, the painful but necessary incorporation of this continent's first peoples into the one body of the Real People, the paternal imperative, in Macdonald's words, "to wean them by slow degrees, from their nomadic habits, which have almost become an instinct, and by slow degrees to absorb them." A man who believed that, every bit as much as a man who believed in the world revolution, could smile and smile, and be a villain.

Nothing is excused here. Willful ignorance is still willful. Dropping the smile, and changing it for tears, does not resurrect the dead. In fact, as Nishnaabeg scholar Leanne Betasamosake Simpson points out, tears can do less than nothing: they can wash the status quo clean. "Canada has become very good at responding to our pain by deploying the politics of grief: a set of tools the state uses to avoid structural changes and accountability by focusing on individual trauma rather than collective, community, or nation-based losses. . . . The politics of grief can also so easily become the politics of distraction."

We know the quality of grief, like the quality of faith, by its fruits. A grief that is individualized and sentimentalized will not bear much fruit at all; as Simpson argues, that impotence is precisely the point. A grief that is "nation-based"—that truly sees the crime of the residential schools as the crime of ethnic cleansing—might bear more. As a minimal step, a more fruitful grief can confirm the conviction that there is no Real People here. And then we can ask what follows from that absence.

———

Over roughly the same period as the Canadian refounding, the United States entered into a parallel, transformative period centred on the 1964 Civil Rights Act, the 1965 Voting Rights Act, and the 1965 Immigration Act—a period sometimes described as America's Second Reconstruction.

It's an apt term. Like the First Reconstruction, in the wake of the Civil War, it was an attempt to overcome the political legacies of slavery, to build a multiracial democracy in the ruins of white rule. Like the First Reconstruction, it was a centralizing and universalizing project, with the righteous end of incorporating more Americans into the Declaration's "all men are created equal" and the Constitution's "We the People," with federal power brought to bear against the state-level oligarchies that stood in the way. And like the First Reconstruction, it was massively resisted and at least partially defeated by those oligarchies. Its legacy is a profound vision of American citizenship; its legacy is also today's deep polarization and unresolved struggle.

In describing the Canadian refounding as an effort to do away with a single, sovereign people, and the American refounding as an effort to reform and renew the sovereign people, I'm certainly painting in broad brushstrokes. On the one hand, Canada saw its own struggles

against racial segregation and disenfranchisement, as I'm
reminded every time I handle a ten-dollar bill bearing the
face of Viola Desmond; on the other, the United States is
unquestionably a product of *métissage* or *mestizaje*. But
which of these themes have become the dominant ones
in their respective political cultures? Which have consistently set the terms of political debate? Just as multinationalism has become the dominant Canadian theme,
the dominant American theme has been the struggle to
extend principles that are conceived as universal.

The official, mainstream statements of American
purpose—the kind that end up inscribed on monuments and printed in passports—bear this out. Speaking
at the 1963 March on Washington, Martin Luther King
Jr. set the historical scene in these terms: "When the architects of our republic wrote the magnificent words of
the Constitution and the Declaration of Independence,
they were signing a promissory note to which every
American was to fall heir." The founding words, and
their idea of a rational and creedal basis of citizenship,
were good and right. Millions of Americans had been
defrauded of their stake in those words and all they
promised, but soon they would receive their fair share
from what King called "the bank of justice." This is the
King that America chose to canonize: not the enemy of
capitalism and militarism, but the prophet of essential
American goodness and its eventual perfection. Several generations on, that is the consensus liberal view
of American history. The American story, as President
Obama reminded his listeners in his farewell address, is

"a constant widening of our founding creed to embrace all and not just some."

At the time King's words were spoken, both Canada and the United States were embarking on progressive, emancipatory projects. But those projects, more than has usually been recognized, took them in very different directions. In Canada, liberation became synonymous with recognizing its "nations within"; in America, liberation became synonymous with marginalizing them.

This is true in two senses. In one, the integrationist and universalizing mainstream of the Second Reconstruction largely displaced a competing vision, in which integration was either impossible or undesirable. This is the Black nationalism of such figures as Marcus Garvey, late-period Du Bois, and Malcom X. Du Bois's entanglement with the civil rights movement offers an especially telling suggestion of paths not taken. As early as the 1930s, while he was at work reshaping the historical memory of Reconstruction, he was also outlining a plan for organized Black consumer power as a means of opting out of the segregated economy. Some three decades later, activists rediscovered *Black Reconstruction* and also embarked on a program of consumer boycotts built on the intellectual foundation that Du Bois had laid out. But Du Bois himself had intended to go much further—towards the establishment of "a Negro nation within a nation," founded on the collective ownership of Black enterprises and on self-governing Black communities. By the time he died in self-imposed exile in Ghana, the day before the March on Washington, he was thoroughly alienated from the mainstream of the civil rights movement. The idea of "a nation within a nation" certainly did not expire with Du Bois, but nor has it ever dislodged the competing vision of perfecting and expanding the nation already in existence.

That vision has also been opposed in the name of a second "nation within": the white South. Southern resistance to the Reconstructions has been both racist *and* nationalist, a duality symbolized by the Confederate flag: an internationally recognized emblem of white supremacy, and the actual standard of a self-declared sovereign state. The tragedy of southern nationalism is that these two strands, self-determination and white supremacy, have been so inextricable. Southern nationalists traditionally understood self-determination not as the power to assert a distinct language, religion, or legal system (as Québécois nationalists have variously conceived of their project), but as the freedom to put white supremacy into effect. Alexander H. Stephens, the vice president and chief ideologist of the Confederacy, did posterity the favour of spelling this out explicitly in the early days of secession: the Confederacy's "foundations are laid, its cornerstone rests upon the great truth, that the negro is not equal to the white man." Three-quarters of a century later, the Senate's leading segregationist, Richard Russell, did us the same favour when he explained why a federal antilynching bill had to go down to defeat: it would "pillory [a] great section of this country before the world as being incapable of its own self-government."

Southern nationalists were quite clear about what

their nationalism was for. So the American struggle against Stephens's "great truth" of racial subordination, and against Russell's ideal of southern "self-government" by lynch law, has also been a struggle to dominate and absorb a rival people. The First Reconstruction's experiment in multiracial democracy grew from the rifle barrels of federal troops. When the occupation was withdrawn under the pressure of domestic terrorism and political indifference, the federal government tacitly restored the white South to autonomy, and to rule by single-party oligarchies. The Second Reconstruction again brought federal power to bear against segregation and disenfranchisement, and it was again resisted under the banner of the Confederacy and in the name of "states' rights." The 2013 rollback of the Voting Rights Act; the renewed voter suppression that it has enabled; the persistence of the partisan polarization driven by the Second Reconstruction, as white southerners gravitated to the Republican Party: all these facts suggest that the struggle remains, if not exactly lost, then much closer to intractable than my parents' generation could have imagined. Sixty years after the high point of the Second Reconstruction, its legacy remains closer to that of the First—a deeply honourable failure—than most Americans would be happy to acknowledge.

America's attempted refounding, then, was not only a struggle to build a multiracial democracy. It was also a struggle to stamp out competing nationalisms, competing senses of belonging and identity, and this was perhaps the more difficult task of the two—if not an impossible task.* In the years since the Second Reconstruction, white southern nationalism has, if anything, metastasized. Its distinctive style of politics—economic oligarchy sanctified by evangelical religion—defines the modern Republican Party and has extended well beyond its original heartland. Its views on abortion and guns set the national agenda. The Southern Strategy capitalized on civil rights backlash to roll back the national welfare state and to empower capital over labour. The Senate filibuster developed as a tool of resistance to civil rights legislation; now, along with the Supreme Court, it enables a sectional veto on national policy reminiscent of the 1850s. Even the more trivial parts of southern culture—Coca-Cola, Krispy Kreme, country music, SEC football—have become thoroughly nationalized. And it is no surprise that the Real People, the Americans entitled to rule even when they are a minority, descends directly from the ruling "white man" celebrated by Stephens.

So when today's American progressives define their adversary as "white nationalism," or "Christian nationalism," they are voicing a truth much more troubling than they seem to recognize. Nationalism is nothing if not tenacious. If the adversary is not a set of policies or beliefs but a competing sense of belonging, albeit a disordered and destructive one, the tools required to over-

---

* It hardly needs to be said that the two nationalisms I have discussed here are not morally equivalent. We might compare white southern nationalism and Black nationalism by transposing some wise words from Machiavelli into a new context: "One will see great desire to dominate in the former, and in the latter only desire not to be dominated."

come it will not be ordinary tools. America might have completed the First Reconstruction by dispossessing the southern planter class and redistributing its plunder. It might, even at this late date, complete the Second Reconstruction by carrying through a program of radical constitutional surgery: for starters, converting the Senate and the Supreme Court into advisory rather than lawmaking bodies. But given the Constitution's deeply and devilishly laid impediments to popular rule, and the Democratic Party's perpetual discomfort with the exercise of power, I cannot imagine that as a realistic future. Unable or unwilling to stamp out the nationalism of the Real People, America seems fated to live with it, and with the perennially recurring possibility of minority rule.

Perhaps the realistically hopeful alternative to that future would look like an American multinationalism—a way of working with the tide of polarization rather than against it. From the perspective of the history I have sketched here, America's contemporary polarization looks something like the return of the repressed. Political "tribalism" confronts the widely shared aspiration for a singular "We the People" with the stubborn, maddening persistence of subnational attachments: party, region, "tribe."

Even as it does little to stop this process of schism, American political culture generally takes its manifest tragedy for granted. Subscribe to a middlebrow American magazine for a year, and you're guaranteed to be offered several dozen think pieces on the woes of hyperpolarization. Tellingly, to conceive the problem in those terms is not to emphasize the egregious things the parties to the divorce are doing (as in the case of the Republican-governed states now moving quickly to cut off abortion access, or to undermine free and fair elections), but rather the sheer fact of the divorce itself. As the journalist George Packer put it, "American politics today requires a word as primal as 'tribe' to get at the blind allegiances and huge passions of partisan affiliation." The premise does not need to be spoken aloud, because it is just common sense: unity (to whatever end) is a great good, and division (for whatever reason) is a great evil. Common sense, in America and elsewhere, is still haunted by the idea of the body politic, the image of the state as an organic unity, a single living being for whom division means dismemberment and therefore death.

But how do new identities come into the world except through such dismemberments? If states are really bodies, maybe they are less like human bodies, hierarchically organized from the head down, jealously guarding their appendages, and more like those slimy, inglorious creatures that can regrow another self from a severed limb.

What if "tribalism" were not a moral failing to be absolved, but simply a hard political fact to be adapted to? What if Americans' "tribal" political affiliations are beginning to resemble ethnicities: deep and relatively fixed sources of identity, nationhood, peoplehood?

If Americans' political identities continue to harden in this way, then the pessimistic scenarios for the future are all too easy to imagine; but a more optimistic scenario might, in fact, look somewhat Canadian. That would be a future of deepening federalism, an increasingly ceremonial central government, legal accommodations for political minorities, and policy set less through national legislation than through subnational negotiations over group rights (for the rights of francophones in Ontario, for instance, substitute the rights of liberals in Texas).

There are signs that such an explicitly multinational settlement might be emerging, even though I don't expect many Americans to be happy about it. I see it in the blue states reinventing themselves as havens of immigration amnesty, strict gun control, and abortion access. I see it in the renewal of Black nationalism out of the equivocal results of the 2020 protests: for instance, in Charles Blow's call for the development of "Black power through Black majorities" in states like Georgia, a political action plan all but explicitly modeled on the historical experience of Quebec. I see it in the social media message Alexandria Ocasio-Cortez posted the day the Supreme Court overturned *Roe v. Wade*: "What I sometimes tell my staff is that the world we are fighting for is already here. It exists in small spaces, places, and communities. . . . So while we can't change the world in a day, we CAN and do have the power to make our own world within our four walls, or our own blocks."

And yet, as much as I value the honest realism in those words—the recognition that the future of the American left looks more like tending one's own garden than storming the barricades—I'm not entirely convinced that a turn to "our own blocks" offers a reasonable way forwards. A multinational settlement would require a truly implausible degree of mutual acquiescence. How long would such a settlement survive the first law dictating jail time for crossing state lines to seek an abortion? How long would California tolerate pockets of gay conversion therapy among its conservative minority? How long would Texas allow the city of Austin to set its own school curriculum? How could Americans accept a multinational future without abandoning a deep-rooted myth about what their country is and where it's going?

And as for America's authoritarians, what Lincoln told them in 1860 is just as true today: "Your purpose, then, plainly stated, is that you will destroy the Government, unless you be allowed to construe and enforce the Constitution as you please, on all points in dispute between you and us. You will rule or ruin in all events."

If Canada's refounding has proved more stable than America's, it is not because Canadians are in any way smarter, wiser, or more virtuous. Above all, it is because the circumstances transmitted from the past set Canada and America very different political tasks. Those circumstances continue to shape Canada's ability to respond to the problem of democratic decline.

What kind of history can Canadians make now? Canada's most important historical accomplishment in the last century was emptying out the category of the Real People. That work grew out of the deep past of Canada's multiple, irreconcilable foundings and out of the modern struggles for Indigenous and French Canadian nationhoods. One result of those struggles—largely unintended, but still highly fortuitous—has been the comparative weakness of the Real People Principle in Canada, at a time when that principle has emerged as a lethal threat to democracy. If the last century's struggles emptied out the Real People, the essential task in this century—at least so far—is keeping it empty. Canadian multiplicity has been a powerful defense for Canadian democracy, and this suggests that leaning into multiplicity can help to insulate Canada against the forces that threaten to undermine democracy here and elsewhere.

With that history in mind, the recent failures of Indigenous reconciliation in Canada are a self-inflicted wound. In 2017, Peter H. Russell wrote that adopting the UN Declaration on the Rights of Indigenous Peoples would "require dealing with the hard stuff: power, money, natural resources. There is no sign yet that dealing with that hard stuff is on the agenda even of a government headed by a prime minister like Justin Trudeau." Four years later, the Trudeau government formally adopted the declaration—and yet there has been precious little action on the "hard stuff" that it entails. Beyond the symbolic actions at which the government excels, it is a truism to describe reconciliation as "stalled."

My suspicion is that this failure has something to do with the implicit assignment of reconciliation to the category of liberal do-goodism: a nice thing to have, a luxury salve for the conscience, but not ultimately a priority on the level of the cost of housing or the price of oil. But reconciliation is *not* merely a nice thing to have: it is a matter of democratic self-defense. It is one of Canada's most powerful tools against authoritarian politics, because of the way it visibly undermines the idea of the Real People.

It doesn't strike me as a coincidence that a recent low point for Indigenous reconciliation, symbolized by the Coastal GasLink standoff in British Columbia and the discovery of the mass graves, was also a recent low point for Canadian democracy, symbolized by the Ottawa occupation and the rise of the populist right. Reconciliation and populism, after all, assume very different models of the political future. On the one hand, complexity: a negotiated patchwork of overlapping claims, histories, and sovereignties. On the other hand, simplicity: one people speaking for one nation in one voice. It shouldn't be surprising that these potential futures are at odds, that reconciliation's loss is populism's gain.

And yet I understand that there is still an essential impasse, in the words of Dale Turner, a leading Indigenous legal theorist, between "Aboriginal nationalists and Canadian sovereigntists." The former object to the claim that Indigenous nations are "within" Canada in any sense at all. Those nations "possess unique forms of rights, sovereignty, and nationhood" that preexist the Canadian state and do not depend on that state for validity. They are better understood as *nations beside* Canada, aspiring to sovereign, nation-to-nation equality, not a more devolved form of colonial rule. "I believe my Ancestors expected the settler state to recognize my nation, our lands, and the political and cultural norms in our territory," writes Leanne Betasamosake Simpson. In this view, the state of the settlers' democracy is not the most pressing concern. Self-government on traditional Indigenous lands is.

I won't pretend to resolve that impasse. But I will suggest that Indigenous nationalists and Canadians invested in the future of democracy share, at least for the moment, a community of interests. We can understand that community abstractly, as in contrasting models of the political future assumed by reconciliation and populism. Or we can understand it concretely, as in the severe damage that authoritarians like Jair Bolsonaro or Donald Trump have done to Indigenous rights in the Americas in recent years. Given those shared interests, Canadian democrats would be well advised to strengthen the Indigenous role in governing Canada. That would not be a substitute for Indigenous self-government—though a Canadian government with a more explicit constitutional role for Indigenous representation would probably make better progress on self-government—but it would be an exercise in democratic self-defense.

A Canadian state that thought in those terms would take *reconciliation* in its literal sense: "taking counsel together again." It might incorporate Indigenous nations into the system of provincial equalization payments. It might ensure Indigenous leaders guaranteed, rather than ad hoc, representation at every provincial first ministers' meeting. It might expand the scope for Indigenous languages in government business—for instance, in the required qualifications for Supreme Court justices. And it might establish dedicated Indigenous parliamentary ridings, drawing on a central lesson of the Trudeau years:

good intentions are no substitute for hard power. "We are Treaty partners," Nishnawbe Aski Nation Grand Chief Alvin Fiddler wrote in a 2017 open letter to the prime minister, amidst a youth suicide crisis in Northern Ontario First Nations. "But we have been legislated into a position where our power is to make proposals and seek program dollars from your bureaucracy." The next time a government promises a "reset" of Indigenous relations, as Trudeau's did in 2015, perhaps it will be more sincere; but it would be something else entirely for that government, especially in a closely divided parliament, to stand or fall on the strength of Indigenous votes. In building a truly multinational parliament for a multinational country, Canada could take inspiration from the Māori electorates in New Zealand or the Uluru Dialogue in Australia—or, indeed, from the de facto quota for parliamentary seats in Quebec, which empowers not only a province but a national minority.

But what happens when the rights of a national minority conflict with the rights of other Canadians? That is a perennial challenge for a multinational democracy, but it has been posed with particular urgency by the CAQ government in Quebec. Its most controversial policies, Bills 21 and 96, would seem to cast the religious expression of Muslims, and the language rights of anglophones and allophones, as an acceptable price to pay for the maintenance of a distinct society. They are something like the assertion of the Real People Principle on a provincial scale.

Over the past several years, I've discovered (anecdotally, at least) that my sympathies for Quebec nationalism run somewhat warmer than those of many anglophones. Perhaps I'm still too much an outsider to feel the right antipathies: the 1995 referendum and all its animosities meant nothing to me at the time, whereas friends who grew up in Ontario can recite to the hundredths place (50.58 percent) the tiny margin that kept Canada whole.

Perhaps my time in Montreal as a postdoc, as brief as it was, triggered a deep memory from childhood Hebrew school: the dogged struggle to keep a minority culture alive for another generation, the sense of endlessly holding entropy at bay, the always incipient guilt—the thought that you yourself could break the thread of a civilization with a wrong step. Once, a friend in Montreal played me Pauline Julien's 1974 recording of "Mommy," a song about a mother who speaks in French to a daughter who can respond only in English: "Mommy, mommy, are you the one to blame?" Many years earlier, when I was sixteen or seventeen, our rabbi brought our Hebrew school confirmation class into the darkened temple sanctuary and read us a short story about the Last Jew, who lives in a furnished habitat in the Smithsonian. Since then, I've known the cold fear of turning into a museum piece, and I've learned something about how to recognize it in others.

Most of all, my memory runs back to a painting I saw in the art museum there, a 1940s Montreal street scene, rain puddles and pedestrians bundled in coats, English signage as far as the eye could see, as if from another world. A revolution really had happened there, in living memory.

Even if it was something as simple as signage, even if my own language was the loser, this was a place where people had collectively changed their world. I thought of Orwell getting off the train in revolutionary Barcelona: "There was much in it that I did not understand, in some ways I did not even like it, but I recognized it immediately as a state of affairs worth fighting for." I think of how hard it seems to collectively change anything about the world we've made—another summer of wildfires, a pandemic we've given up on tracking—and even a sign I can't read strikes me as hopeful.

Of course, revolutions curdle. In time, the social cohesion and sense of shared purpose it takes to make a revolution turn exclusionary and suspicious. The ambition of making another world degenerates into protective fear for the world you've made, and the conservative will to defend it against all comers. Hence, among other things, Bill 21.

Multinational or "pillarized" democracies are hardly immune from right-populism or bigotry. The Netherlands, for generations home to parallel Protestant, Catholic, and socialist civil societies and political parties, has also been home to Pim Fortuyn and Geert Wilders, pioneering anti-immigrant populists of the modern era. Switzerland, the world's oldest multinational democracy, voted in a 2009 referendum to ban the construction of minarets on mosques. The current absence of a single, sovereign people, on which I've pinned much of my hope for Canada, is no guarantee against the resurgence of the Real People Principle or the development of anti-immigration into a political force to be reckoned with.

A plausibly pessimistic future is one in which the CAQ wins more control of immigration policy for Quebec, redoubles its commitment to a *laïcité* that walks, swims, and quacks like Islamophobia, and is echoed on the federal level by a return to the "barbaric cultural practices" playbook. In fact, it's possible to see Bill 21 as an enabler of right-populism in Canada as a whole—the kind of issue on which a future populist leader might make a strategic concession, limiting his or her losses in Quebec and paving the way to a federal plurality or majority. The more space *laïcité* takes up as a central Quebec issue in federal elections, the less room there will be for Quebec to play its long-standing role as a bulwark of social democracy and social liberalism on the federal level.

There would certainly be precedents. In the Dutch and Swiss cases, anti-immigrant populism went some distance towards unifying deeply divided societies. Fortuyn wrote and spoke explicitly about that political goal: uniting a fractured nation against a new enemy, Islam. In Switzerland, the minaret ban was popular across all four official language groups (though less so among francophones). In the face of an immigrant group imagined as sufficiently "other," old differences begin to seem trivial—and whatever stability those old differences offered begins to fall away.

It could happen here, too. And yet Canada's persistent lack of unity still strikes me as at least a potentially saving grace. Bill 21's ban on religious symbols for public employees, along with Bill 96's reduction of anglophone and allophone language rights, is at the centre of the CAQ's cultural project—what it sees as the reinforcement of Quebec's distinct society. Yet that same reinforcement also drives Quebec farther apart from the rest of Canada; it may well have the effect of further entrenching multiculturalism elsewhere, as the feature that defines the rest of Canada against Quebec. The more likely future seems to be one in which Quebec's policies on immigration and minority cultures deepen rather than undermine Canadian multiplicity. It is a future in which those policies, and the attitudes that drive them, live on in a kind of political quarantine.

How long will that quarantine last? I suspect it will last until a majority in Quebec comes to see that *laïcité* is like an invasive species, an idea grounded in the history and struggles of a very different place—that it, not a headscarf, is the threat to their distinct society. And, whether or not they believe me, I am almost as invested in that distinct society as they are. That, I take it, is part of what it means to live in Canada after the refounding: to have a selfish interest in the real flourishing of nations that are not mine.

Chapter 2

CONFEDERATION

IN A 2019 NOVEL, ANDRÉ Alexis describes an annual parade in the fictional Southern Ontario town of Coulson's Hill. Each year, some of the townsfolk dress up as the Fathers of Confederation—"John A. Macdonald, Adams George Archibald, et al."—and board a dozen flatbed trucks. The rest of the townsfolk, dressed in what they imagine to be Indigenous garb, line the parade route and pelt them with rotten fruit in "symbolic restitution" for colonialism. As a tourist draw, the parade is highly lucrative.

Like all satire, this requires a grain or two of truth to be fit for purpose. One grain is the hypocrisy of the liberal guilt that is all too willing to confess someone else's sins for profit. But the other grain is a certain kind of friendly contempt for this country's founders that strikes me as distinctively Canadian. What are founders, after all, but the tallest of tall poppies? The idea of splattering them with tomatoes each year, in exchange for tourist dollars and faux reconciliation, seems to be at least in the realm of plausibility, which is where good satire lives.

Something of the same spirit marks the recent defacements of Macdonald statues in Charlottetown, Montreal, Hamilton, and Kitchener-Waterloo. That's not to say that the defacers lacked seriousness of purpose, but that the rest of us have difficulty taking the vandalism completely seriously, because we have difficulty taking Macdonald completely seriously. The statues are repaired, or they aren't, and condemnatory plaques are grafted on, or they aren't, and some *tut-tuts* issue from various political offices, or they don't. And meanwhile in America, entire running battles in the culture wars are fought over the fate of monuments to Confederate generals whose only accomplishment was treason—let alone the fate of monuments to the country's actual founders.

Few things are more foreign to Canada than the intensity of feeling with which Americans regard their founders. There is the near-religious reverence that the founders themselves sought and cultivated, that they in their more self-aware moments understood themselves to be seeking: "Men of the most exalted genius and active minds are generally most perfect slaves to the love of fame," the young John Adams wrote in his diary; Alexander Hamilton spoke of "the love of fame, the ruling passion of the noblest minds." Like many in their generation, they took for granted the Enlightenment theory that held the gods worshipped in antiquity to be deified mortals, raised into the pantheon in honour of some great

Confederation

service to their people. Who was to say that it couldn't happen again?

And coexisting with the founders' legend, which has been handed down from Parson Weems to Lin-Manuel Miranda, there is the deep and personal outrage of the kind that comes from discovering that you have been betrayed by your hero, or your father. Jefferson's meticulous ledgers of slave-breeding, or Washington's relentless pursuit of the fugitive slave Ona Judge, sting in the way that only the most powerful disillusionment can—not despite their greatness, but because of it.

As early as 1838, a young Abraham Lincoln described the cult of the founders as America's "political religion." And so it is: try Mount Rushmore on the Fourth of July—shells bursting over the pharaonic heads of presidents, graven at eighty times the size of life. The alternative to this god-haunted politics is generally not indifference, but bitter atheism. For a sense of the atheism, try Gore Vidal's 1973 historical novel of the founding, *Burr*, where the ruling image for Washington is the cold-blooded snake:

> Washington gave the child that cold dull serpent's glance he usually reserved for those private soldiers who were about to be flogged. . . .
> The decorous relationship with his wife Martha was simply an alliance between properties, and typical of Washington's ambition, of his cold serpent's nature. . . .
> His powerful will and serpentine cunning

79

made of a loose confederation of sovereign states a strong federal government graven to this day in Washington's sombre Roman imperial image.

There is a seriousness of disgust here that can only be a backhanded compliment to greatness. Washington and the others would not be worthy objects of disgust if they had not in fact succeeded in making a nation in their image. Vidal's narrator (Aaron Burr, the son of a dynasty of Puritan ministers) knew his Bible, and Vidal knew that he knew: "Thou shalt not make unto thee any graven image. . . . Thou shalt not bow down thyself to them, nor serve them." The implication, as old as the Decalogue and as recent as Watergate, is clear enough: if they were idol-makers, then the country itself is the idol. The relevant sin here is not only slavery, as evil as it was, but greatness itself—an inhuman, Miltonic ambition that was nevertheless wildly successful. The American founders were revolutionaries, makers of something truly new, but like a thousand kings and emperors before them, they wanted to be venerated after their death. And so, more or less, they are.

Could you imagine writing something similar about John A. Macdonald or George-Étienne Cartier, except as farce? No more than you could imagine writing it (and here I'm choosing randomly from a list of current cabinet ministers) about Anita Anand or Bill Blair. The Fathers of Confederation are decidedly of the same species as Canada's contemporary political class. Conversely, the accomplishment of the American founders, and the political religion that developed in their wake, renders them distant and alien figures.

America's political structure was built by demigods. Canada's was built by politicians. As those structures come under increasing pressure, Canada's unheroic, unmonumental past comes more and more to look like a democratic asset.

———

"A Canadian," said Northrop Frye, "is an American who rejects the Revolution."

At first, I read that line as granting somewhat more similarity than I'd prefer: Canadians and Americans are interchangeable, save for some old political differences. But on a second reading, the line looks more audacious. Frye is claiming that Canadians are just as entitled to think of themselves as Americans—that is, as inheritors of a long-standing political tradition on the American continents—as are citizens of the United States. The United States, as much as its people might think otherwise, has no monopoly on the history of this shared place. Others, who are every bit of this place as they are, actively reject their most central myth.*

———

* In this respect, Frye's line is identical in structure to George-Étienne Cartier's famous quip to Queen Victoria: "A French-Canadian is an Englishman who speaks French." As the historian Christopher Moore observes, "It seemed like a cringing plea from a self-abasing *Canadien* ashamed of his origins. Cartier, however, meant it as a challenge, almost a taunt. His British audiences of lords and gentlemen—and Queen Victoria herself—mostly

What does it mean to reject the revolution? One long-standing interpretation of that rejection says that Canadians are, by culture and habit, all the adjectival opposites of "revolutionary": conservative, cautious, deferential, the pale Tory shadows of the dynamic, egalitarian Americans.

Certainly there is some truth there, though perhaps less than national stereotypes might suggest. For instance, to put "egalitarian" on the American side of the ledger is to ignore the egalitarian practices of Indigenous nations that shaped political life in Canada for generations before its formal founding. It is to ignore, as well, the radicalism of Canada's nineteenth-century reformers and democrats, and the fact that Canada has for decades outperformed the United States (though it has underperformed the Nordic countries) on measures of social and economic equality.

More generally, it is all too easy to wander into vague generalities about national characters, hard to prove or disprove, always subject to example and counterexample, as long as we think of "revolution" as some sort of transhistorical state of mind.

But "revolution" is not a personality trait. It is a process, an event, a thing that happened or did not. Past revolutions shape the present through the institutions they tear down and build up—but also, and just as important,

---

understood hostility to France and all things French as part of the birthright of a true Englishman. They must have been taken aback to hear one who spoke French as his mother tongue dare to call himself an Englishman and their equal."

through the sorts of political conduct they set up as memorable, honourable, normative. To exaggerate just a little, a revolution's monuments—in stone and metal, but also in story and myth—*are* the revolution. A successful revolution becomes a mental model of how political change takes place, even long after the revolution has passed.

To say that Canadians are Americans who reject the revolution, then, is to say that Canadians reject the mental model of change that the revolution entails—and that they find their own normative model of change elsewhere, in a different set of events, a quite different political "origin story." It is not that sweeping, dramatic changes have never taken place north of the 49th parallel (a number of those changes were the subject of the last chapter). Rather, the pivotal event of the American myth, the Revolution of 1776, has no Canadian counterpart, and this is more than a historical curiosity.

Rejecting the revolution, and continuing to reject it, strengthens Canadian democracy in the present. It means rejecting the demigod charisma that adheres to successful revolutionaries, and, conversely, embracing the unheroic possibilities of ordinary politics.

In the last chapter, I discussed the Real People Principle and the way that it enables minority rule: the way that membership in the right racial or religious group can, in the reactionary imagination, confer political power that sheer numbers cannot. For much of the American right, and for a growing segment of the Canadian right, as well, the Real People Principle offers ideological heft and patriotic plausibility to claims of election fraud and stolen votes, to instruments of minority rule like the US Senate and Supreme Court, and to the idea that multiracial democracy is inherently suspect. It is powerful not because it is explicitly authoritarian, but because it is clothed in the language and symbols of democracy. It can practice mass disenfranchisement while smugly asking, as Andrew Johnson rhetorically asked Frederick Douglass, "Do you deny that first great principle of the right of the people to govern themselves?"

That combination—the gestures of democracy and the practices of disenfranchisement—is the foundation of modern authoritarianism. It negates popular rule, and, just as dangerously, elevates and acclaims a singular leader.

For all their demotic and commonsensical trappings, for all their stylistic commitment to what the political theorist Pierre Ostiguy calls "flaunting the low," contemporary populist movements are not really of or by the people in any meaningful sense. To name a populist movement is often to name the singular leader who is synonymous with it: Trumpism, Orbánism, Chavismo. Their images become ideologies. Their whims become party platforms (sometimes literally: in lieu of voting on the usual convention platform in 2020, the Republican Party simply passed a resolution stating that it "will continue to enthusiastically support the President's America-first agenda"). Their personal corruption is taken as a triumphal act of getting one over on a corrupt system. Populism is personalism.

Where does this political paradox come from? Why, across continents and contexts, are these movements so populist in theory, and so antipopular in practice?

Maybe, if the Real People truly are besieged—by a hostile majority, by immigrants, by global elites, by the deep state—it makes sense to take refuge under the wing of a powerful protector. Populist authoritarianism, then, would be a kind of wartime leadership for domestic politics, the pragmatic reaction of those who see their power and status as existentially endangered. Donald Trump made his pitch to white evangelicals in just those terms: "I will tell you, Christianity is under tremendous siege," he told a 2016 audience at a Christian college in Iowa. But under a Trump presidency, "Christianity will have power. If I'm there, you're going to have plenty of power, you don't need anybody else." Florida governor Ron DeSantis, Trump's rival and potential successor, closed out the 2022 election campaign with an ad that announced his divine anointment: "And on the eighth day, God looked down on His planned paradise and said, 'I need a protector.' So God made a fighter."

Or maybe populist movements have no better way of making decisions—of choosing the priorities and trade-offs and compromises that necessarily come with power—than entrusting them to a singular decider. After all, "the people"—even if taken in the more limited sense of the Real People—is a tremendously broad group, with few immediately obvious common interests. Those disparate interests might be built into a common program, but much of the insurgent appeal of populism lies in its militant contempt for the deliberative practices and institutions that make such building possible. Populist movements, then, might turn to a powerful leader almost by default, having burned their other bridges to collective decision-making. In Trump's most ominous words from the 2016 election, "I alone can fix it." Populism almost invariably ends up at that same "I alone."

But there is something else essential to keep in mind: democracy and authoritarian leadership are not as antithetical as we would like to believe. In combining the language of democracy and the dominance of singular leaders, today's authoritarian populist movements build on a long and powerful tradition. Since the revolutions of the eighteenth century, democracy has always made room for highly personalized, charismatic forms of leadership, especially at moments of crisis. The age of revolutions, as the historian David A. Bell reminds us, was also an age of "men on horseback": founders who won power through personal charisma, popular acclamation, and military prowess. In this view, Washington was not only an American figure but a global one, a commander and redeemer whose most relevant peers include Simón Bolívar in Venezuela, Toussaint Louverture in Haiti, and Napoléon Bonaparte in France.

In a more secure democratic era, the repeated turn from popular uprisings to charismatic rule might have seemed more puzzling—an aberration, a stubborn glitch in the program. But in this age of democratic decline, as Bell argues, the contradiction appears less glaring. These days, it hardly seems to be a contradiction at all:

> It is at moments like the present that we are forced to confront the reality that charismatic authoritarianism in no sense represents a backsliding, an atavistic and presumably temporary return to the days of warlords and kings, before the onward march of liberal democracy continues. A potentially authoritarian charisma is as modern a phenomenon as any of the liberal ideas and practices that arose in the age of revolution, including human rights and democratic republicanism and constitutional government.

Of course, Washington, who ended his career in voluntary retirement rather than enforced exile, was not exactly a Napoléon. But contemporaries sometimes found an uncanny likeness in the two military heroes. Looking back at Washington's elevation from successful general to national saviour, his successor John Adams wrote, "Something of the same kind has occurred in France and has produced a Napoleon and his Empire."

The great revolutions of the eighteenth century produced something more lasting than empires: those mental models of change, those templates for heroic political action that have been taken up in every generation since. It was almost too on the nose when Hugo Chávez literally dug up Bolívar's bones—but in one way or another,

politicians have been exhuming their revolutionary predecessors for more than two centuries.

In the United States, as in Latin America, the struggle for (white) self-government was also an armed
struggle against a foreign occupier. It is easy enough to
conflate these two kinds of freedom—the freedom of
self-government, and the freedom of home rule—and
indeed they often are conflated, in Independence Day
celebrations, in the iconography of the founders, and in
the myth of the Revolution. But these are very different
kinds of freedom, and one does not entail the other. It is
just as possible for foreign rule to be replaced with a local
dictatorship—the story of many of the postcolonial regimes of the twentieth century. But in the United States,
the expulsion of the British really did go hand in hand
with a new, if limited, experiment in democracy.

To speak in the rough sense in which myths operate,
Americans really did win their democracy at gunpoint.
Democracy really did require heroic acts of violence and
the successful defiance of an imperial power.

Ever since, political violence has held a privileged
place in the American imagination. No society is immune to political violence, but it matters whether that
violence is concordant or discordant with the national
myth. Where it is concordant, violence does not simply bubble up from the margins—it takes an honoured
place at the centre of power. Think of the Revolution-era
trappings of far-right groups from the KKK to the Oath
Keepers and Three Percenters. Think of the way the experience of the Revolution licenses a federally sanctioned

gun culture. "What the Stuarts had tried to do to their political enemies [seize their guns], George III had tried to do to the colonists," wrote Justice Scalia in the 2008 Supreme Court decision that established an individual right to bear arms.

Or think of the universal habit of referring to the president as "commander in chief." In theory, "commander in chief" refers to the president's constitutional role as head of the military, not to the president in his civilian capacity. In practice, it is the title Americans reach for when the occasion demands an especially exalted form of address for the head of government—on the evident assumption that no title is finally more exalted than that of war leader.

And that fact points to an important truth, not about Americans in particular, but about authority in general: there are few forms of charisma more powerful or more enduring than that won through the successful application of violence against one's enemies. (Even the Jesus of the Gospels, who ought to be a prime example of nonviolent charisma in Western literature, won his popular authority by forcibly casting out demons—through convincing displays of violence.) That is the ultimate source of the original charisma won by the American founders: not only the creation of a republic, but the violent wresting away of a republic from an empire. That is the source, as well, of the subsidiary charisma claimed by the politicians who still use Washington's old military title, still speak (again, literally) in the monumental shadows of the founders, and still call on the drama and bloodshed of the

Revolutionary era to justify every American's right to be fearsomely armed.

I think, in this context, about paths not taken: for instance, about Benjamin Franklin's 1754 proposal that the American colonies elect representatives to the British Parliament, or about William Pitt's last-ditch effort in 1775 to forestall war by persuading Parliament to recognize colonial self-government and legalize the Continental Congress. Either proposal would have likely set the American colonies on a gradual path to self-rule, but in neither case would self-rule have been a prize of war. And in neither case, I'd speculate, would the model of American political leadership harbour quite such authoritarian potential, as it does in so many countries shaped by a revolution's legacy.

That alternate history is somewhat closer to the real nineteenth-century history lived out by Canada. No doubt its history is largely as violent as that of any settler colony—and even among the settlers themselves, Canada's pivotal years of democratization, the 1830s and 1840s, were years of rebellion and riot. The idea of Canada as the "peaceable kingdom" would be alien to Poundmaker or Big Bear, to Papineau or Mackenzie. And yet the distinct way that Canada came to be self-governing matters in some profound ways for its political culture today.

In Canada's history, it matters that democracy and national independence were dissociated. That is, the provinces that would become Canada began to democratize well before Confederation, and well before gaining full autonomy from the British Empire (a process that could not be considered complete until 1931, or even 1982).

Democracy and independence were the result of different processes, carried out by different sets of leaders. The founders of Canadian democracy did good and important work—but it was not freighted with the achievement of full national independence, and it was not burdened with the kind of authority that can be won only at gunpoint. They were often principled, occasionally courageous, sometimes petty, but they were not conquering warriors. They were politicians.

One such politician was Louis-Hippolyte LaFontaine. In his 1840 manifesto for democracy, the "Address to the Electors of Terrebonne," which was printed and distributed across Upper and Lower Canada, in French and English, the essential link is not between democracy and independence, but between political liberty and social equality. "Without political liberty we have no future; our needs cannot be satisfied. . . . They can deny us this status only if they are able to destroy the social equality [*Pour nous empêcher d'en jouir, il faudrait détruire l'égalité sociale*] which constitutes the distinctive characteristic as much of the population of Upper Canada as of Lower Canada. . . . No privileged caste, beyond and above the mass of the people, can exist in Canada."

There had long been a productive exchange of ideas between Canadian and American democrats: in 1837 and 1838, for instance, the rebellions in Upper and Lower Canada were launched with manifestos modeled on the American Declaration of Independence. Nevertheless, I'd suggest that LaFontaine's words are politically productive in ways that Jefferson's are not.

Take the identity of the *they* who would destroy social equality in the Canadas. (In the original French, the verb is impersonal: more literally, "one would have to destroy . . ."). In fact, the target of the argument is not a distant royal bogeyman, but something much nearer to hand: the local oligarchs who monopolized political offices and economic power. Democracy is not simply a matter of casting out the foreigner—or even the Anglo Canadians, given LaFontaine's pivotal collaborations with the Upper Canada reformers—but of restraining and counterbalancing unchecked economic power. LaFontaine wanted to vindicate the right of Canadians, not the British Crown, to choose Canada's leaders; but the local struggle took priority. (In this respect, the then-radical claim of Lord Durham's 1838 report had been correct: colonial self-government and separation from the empire were distinct questions.)

Why, according to LaFontaine, do we need democracy in the first place? For a reason as prosaic as it is critical: so that our needs can be satisfied. In this powerful formulation, the counterpart of liberty is not foreign rule but domestic oligarchy, the concentration of power in the hands of the wealthy and incestuously connected few, whose ruling factions went by the name of the Family Compact in Upper Canada and the Château Clique in Lower Canada. One typical oligarch, in the words of a later historian, "was an executive councillor, a legislative councillor, President of the Toronto and Lake Huron Railroad, Governor of the British American Fire and Life Assurance Company and President of the Board of

Trade." As long as the needs of such a man were so lavishly satisfied, the bulk of Canadians' needs could not be. The accuracy of description—*what* democracy is for—contributes to an accuracy of diagnosis: *who* threatens it, and *why*. On the other hand, the remaining flaw in LaFontaine's formulation, his inattention to the way his version of social equality depends on the expropriation of native land, is symptomatic of most nineteenth-century democrats. Democracy would unlock "the well-being promised us by America's vast nature"; by now, we can imagine what *that* means.

Still, there is something important in LaFontaine's concrete requirements for the achievement of political liberty. These requirements include such familiar elements as public consent to taxation and to the laws, as expressed by freely elected representatives. But they also include the people's "efficient participation in the action of its government, its legitimate influence in turning the gears of administration, and its effective and constitutional control of the individuals more immediately appointed to operate this administration." Those demands could be satisfied under a system of "responsible government."

Responsible government is a term of art originating in the British parliamentary system. It means that government ministers are responsible to—or serve at the pleasure of—the legislature. When that legislature is popularly elected, then the ministers who run the government are under popular control. But for much of British history, ministers were creatures of the king. Parliament could rail against them, could on rare occasions impeach them, but for the most point had to put up with them. In Britain, ministers' accountability to Parliament was established slowly and haphazardly: as late as 1762, being a royal favourite was enough to qualify you for the job of prime minister; as late as 1834, the king could still fire the prime minister on his own initiative. An elected legislature authorized to tax but not spend, with decisive power in the hands of royal governors and their appointed councils: that was where the Province of Canada (formed from the union of Upper and Lower Canada in 1840) lingered through 1848, when LaFontaine and his colleague Robert Baldwin finally secured the colony's first fully responsible government.

Three things about their success stand out. First, it was not a Promethean matter of designing an entirely new experiment in self-government, but a rewiring of the connections of a system that was already in place. Before 1848, there was a queen, a governor-general, an executive council, and a colonial legislature; after 1848, there was a queen, a governor-general, an executive council, and a colonial legislature. The difference is that power now flowed through this system in new directions, and through newly pivotal nodes (despite the fact that voting rights in Canada were still restricted to propertied men). LaFontaine and Baldwin understood democracy in terms of "participation . . . influence . . . and control": not an either/or, not a stark matter of abolishing governments that trample on rights, but as a continuum, a way of opening channels through which popular power can flow.

Second, their achievement was a *political* achievement, won through popular pressure, community organizing, and parliamentary maneuvering. The pivotal moments included elections in the face of mob violence and Orange Order bigotry, Baldwin's legislative success in embarrassing the minority Tories into endorsing his resolutions on responsible government, and the governor-general's 1848 decision to back down in the face of a strong parliamentary majority. The struggle demanded and rewarded courage, moral as well as physical, but not to a dramatically different extent than the political struggles of our own time: no battlefields, no cavalry charges. The moment of greatest trial for the new ministry, when anti-French rioters burned down the parliament building in Montreal, was a matter of stoically enduring violence rather than successfully inflicting it. Lin-Manuel Miranda is not going to write a musical about responsible government.

Third, the newly democratized government almost immediately set about using its power, as LaFontaine had promised, to satisfy economic need. For instance, it financed a "railroad boom" that would help to grow Canada's rail network by more than thirtyfold between 1850 and 1864. That is the sort of ambitious, disruptive infrastructure program that an oligarchic government could just as easily fund in theory, but would be far less likely to support in practice—because of the way it threatened to displace incumbent economic interests, including those of the ruling oligarchs themselves. The Canadian oligarchs had rational, self-interested reasons for keeping a firm lid on economic growth, and the population growth that came with it: they preferred a relatively stronger position in a smaller, poorer society to a relatively weaker position in a larger, richer one. Canadian democrats' reasons to break their power were similarly rational and similarly self-interested, though in a far more expansive sense: they understood that a democratic society was, in LaFontaine's words, "the goal essential to our prosperity."

What they left to subsequent Canadians was not only a more democratic government, but also a lasting model of change-making: one in which self-government was secured through the ordinary arts of politics and set to the ordinary ends of prosperity and growth. They did their work with an unusual degree of creativity, principle, and tolerance, but nothing they did seems otherworldly or out of reach. Three years after securing responsible government, the Baldwin-LaFontaine ministry collapsed, for the usual reasons of coalitional infighting. Of course it did.

———————

What the American founders accomplished *does* seem out of reach. It is not simply that their achievements were imbued with the glamour of violence, but that they took place in an alien world—one that is distant from us in mood, climate, and spirit, as much as in time. This is more than the gulf of historical retrospect. The founders themselves often expressed the sense that they spoke from an older order of things—an order that might or might not have been dying, but one that certainly appeared out of step with the country that was being born.

Ten years after the colonies declared independence, George Washington wrote to a friend: "What astonishing changes a few years are capable of producing. . . . From the high ground we stood upon, from the plain path which invited our footsteps, to be so fallen! so lost! it is really mortifying." Benjamin Rush saw Americans, not long after the Revolution, "devouring each other like beasts of prey." George Clymer saw a politics increasingly dominated by "men of narrow souls and no natural interest in the society." James Madison arrived at the Virginia state legislature to find not enlightened statesmen, but only politicians with "a particular interest to serve," who spent their time in "crudeness and tedious discussion."

This was more than ordinary grumbling: the divide they perceived was very real. It was a divide between the old model of classical republicanism and the commercial, horse-trading, interest-ridden world that was coming into being. The old model took its inspiration from the republics of the ancient world, and from their accomplishments that (in the words of Montesquieu, the founders' most-cited philosopher) "astonish our small souls." Central to those accomplishments was a demanding ideal of liberty, in which the only individual who was truly free was one who was untouched by arbitrary power, and who had no dependence on others. Republicanism had a radical strand, a suspicion of established authority and a zeal to extend the material conditions of liberty beyond a narrow elite. But many of the founders, who held that a republic should be led by its educated and propertied gentlemen, saw no contradiction in a liberty whose economic base rested on slavery (didn't Rome's?), a liberty that would be most fully enjoyed by a relative few. A republic was a society governed by such men, motivated by civic virtue and public spirit, and above all disinterested: so secure in their material needs that they could accurately perceive and fairly implement the common good.

Some of the distance between that mental world and ours, observed the historian Gordon Wood, is summed up in the fact that we've largely forgotten the meaning of the word *disinterested*: when we use it at all, it's as an accidental synonym for *uninterested*. While we can easily conceive of not caring about an issue, "we cannot quite imagine someone who is capable of rising above a pecuniary interest and being unselfish and unbiased where an interest might be present." But that was precisely how many of the American founders saw themselves.

And if this belief was often false and self-serving—as their political opponents never tired of pointing out—it was also sincerely held, powerfully influential, and backed by history's most honoured precedents. The American founders did not stop imagining themselves into the role of classical heroes when the Revolutionary War was over. They put on the imaginary togas again when they came to write the new republic's constitution, conceding a limited role for popular participation, but for the most part establishing a government of gentlemen, insulated from public pressure. Their federal constitution would be decidedly less democratic than most of the existing state constitutions. Its structure would protect the republic from the evils that Madison enumerated in the famous *Federalist No. 10*: "a rage for paper money, for an abolition of debts, for an equal division of property, or for any other improper or wicked project."

The founders' undemocratic Constitution continues to stifle American politics right up to the current day. In the last chapter, I discussed some of the ways in which its dead hand still hangs on the present. Yet surely some of its implausible endurance stems from the fact that there has rarely ever been an ideal of politics more tantalizing than the one offered by the founders. At times, it seems as if contemporary American politics is just an organized, collective yearning for that impossible ideal. That ideal of disinterested civic virtue is there in the American exasperation with parties and partisanship (what are parties but organized interests?), in political fictions from *Mr. Smith Goes to Washington* to *Bulworth*, John McCain's "Straight Talk Express" and Joe Biden's "No Malarkey," and even in Trump's farcical promise to serve as president without a salary.

As much as the founders attempted to embed that ideal in the republic they made, they were, as Wood persuasively argues, fighting a losing, rearguard action. The place America was becoming was wildly out of step with their ruling vision: commercial, not aristocratic; luxury-seeking, not self-denying; governed by parties, not consensus; the free-for-all of industrial capitalism, not the purportedly ordered liberty of the classical republics.

Americans are left with a set of idols who barely resemble them: Egyptian gods with the heads of birds and jackals. Americans are left, writes Wood, "with our despairing effort to make them one with us, to close that terrifying gap that always seems to exist between them and us. Nevertheless, in our hearts we know that they are not one with us, that they are separated from us, as they were separated from every subsequent generation of Americans, by an immense cultural chasm."* We will not see their like again, because the world is so changed. Their like is impossible now.

No such chasm separates Canadians from the founders who established "a new Nationality" in British North America. Even in something as superficial as dress, the Fathers of Confederation are moderns: with a slight update to their neckties and the cut of their coats, they would be indistinguishable in a crowd on Bay Street. More to the point, the negotiations that established modern Canada

---

* Of course, Wood's interpretation of the classical republican roots of the American founding is very much a contested one, and it is not as central to the field of early-American history as it once was. I'm drawing on it here because it offers the best explanation I'm aware of for that persistent Oedipal mood in American politics, which has been so striking to me as a participant and observer. Maybe this is idiosyncratic to me, but I think we need to account for the felt distance between the founders and the present to understand Americans' continued failure to displace them in national memory. Histories that put the emphasis on the qualities of the founders with which it is easier to identify (e.g., their liberal individualism, or their sheer, grubby self-interest) cannot account for that distance in the same way.

took place in a recognizably modern world—*this* world, the world we still inhabit—of mass media, parliamentary bargaining, and, above all, political parties. For the American founders, the emergence of parties (even the ones that they themselves helped to create) was a grave shock. They still had at least one foot in the premodern understanding of *party* as synonymous with *faction*, a quasi-conspiracy designed to exploit the state for private ends. They assumed that enlightened statesmen would be as independent of party pressure and patronage as they were of material want; the fact that they were not came as a foundational loss of innocence.

If Canadian politics ever passed through a similar loss, it was well in the past by the time the delegates convened in Charlottetown and Quebec City in 1864. The negotiations aimed at the goal of broad consensus—but what mattered was a consensus of parties, not statesmen. From the unity government that represented the Province of Canada, to the Maritime delegates from both government and opposition benches, it was assumed that Confederation would be savaged by any parties that were excluded (and so it was, by the few parties that were, including the Parti Rouge of Canada East).

Before the ink on the agreement had dried, delegates acknowledged that calculation openly. "Politicians are generally cunning fellows," Prince Edward Island delegate Edward Whelan wrote for publication in 1865, "and those in the several Maritime governments showed this quality to great advantage when they appointed members of the opposition to aid them in perfecting the great scheme of confederation, because if the people of the several provinces should be so unwise as to complain . . . the opposition would have to bear the censure as well as those in the administration." He could have easily said the same of the three-party coalition that negotiated on behalf of the Province of Canada. Confederation was an exercise in partisan logrolling, and the delegates generally did not display any kind of Madisonian embarrassment with that fact— that was, in the end, their profession and their calling.

Moreover, the parties to which they were accountable were in the process of transforming into modern, mass-membership parties, with all the apparatus of organizing, from party newspapers to torchlight rallies. The Confederation delegates, heirs of the responsible government struggle of the 1840s, were seeking an agreement that could ultimately be sold to those mass memberships. That does not mean that Confederation was a thoroughly democratic process: Canada's provincial parliament did not call a new election before approving Confederation, and the rejection of Leonard Tilley's pro-Confederation government in New Brunswick failed to derail the project. Still, the Fathers of Confederation had to account for mass constitutional politics in a way that campaigners for the Charlottetown Accord or Brexit or a new Chilean constitution would have immediately recognized. George Brown, for instance, kept a keen eye on the possibility of mass street protests against Confederation; that they did not materialize, his Toronto newspaper argued, was a sign of public support, or at least acquiescence. When ordinary members of Brown's or

Macdonald's parties identified themselves as, say, Grits or Tories, they were making the kind of statement that would have been literally unintelligible in the previous century, when party membership was reserved for elites engaged in high politics in parliament or at court. The fact that that kind of statement *is* intelligible to us suggests, again, that we stand on the same side of the divide.

That Confederation was so widely acceptable to those parties and their memberships has led a number of historians to conclude that it was a project without ideology, and even largely without principle. Few grand ideas, few references to Montesquieu or Tacitus, were necessary to justify an exercise in pure bargaining among a set of very worldly men. "Peace, order, and good government" made a pithy slogan for the new union, but it could equally well have read "Land, railroads, and sound currency." And while politicians are always capable of dressing up the division of spoils in the language of principle (that being one of the job requirements), the Fathers of Confederation were not especially hard pressed in that regard: the nature of parliamentary government, and the multipartisan structure of the negotiations, ensured that whatever they agreed would very likely be ratified by the provinces. They had the votes, and they knew it. Perhaps as a result, the public debates on Confederation did not rise to anything like a world-historical standard.

Nevertheless, there *were* issues of principle at stake — and if they seem so ordinary and workaday, maybe it is because they are still so familiar. Think of how easy it is to imaginatively transpose to our time the polarized gridlock and dysfunction that brought the Province of Canada to a political standstill, and that seemed to demand a new constitution. When the young MP Richard Cartwright spoke in the Confederation debates of the "bitterness and virulence of party feeling, and the narrowness and acrimony to which those feelings give rise," he might as well have been speaking yesterday. When Reformers demanded "rep by pop" to bring democratic power into line with demographic reality, they might have been complaining about today's shambles of first-past-the-post voting. When Cartier's Bleus demanded constitutional protection for *"notre langue, notre religion, et nos lois,"* they spoke to Quebec's perpetual identity politics in a way that would not have sounded out of place in the Bill 21 debate. Polarization, fair representation, identity, federalism—the issues that structure politics to this day, hashed out in 1864 by modern politicians in modern terms. (Though note that the Indigenous nations do not figure in this list of issues at all, as they barely figured in the Confederation debates. The addition of Indigenous issues to the permanent agenda of Canadian politics is one reason why Canada's twentieth-century changes constitute a refounding.)

Cult objects thrive on distance, desire, and mystery; it is hard to have a cult of the familiar. But Confederation *is* familiar, almost the product of living memory rather than the product of a heroic age. It is difficult to imagine a cult of Confederation. By contrast, the distance of the American founding lends itself to worship. There very much *is* a cult of the Constitution and the founding: the tricorn hats of the Tea Party protestors railing against universal health care; the divinely inspired founding as preached by fundamentalists like Cleon Skousen and Glenn Beck; Trump's "1776 Project," a slapdash committee report intended to sand down slavery's role in American history. It is not a coincidence that the cult of the founding is mostly a reactionary project—a cult centred on an old, dead object, and the thinking of the day long ago when that object was alive and vital.* Recall Richard Russell from the last chapter, the southern senator who claimed that an antilynching bill would violate his people's "self-government." Russell led and met regularly with a powerful Senate bloc of segregationist Democrats—except they weren't called that. They were called "Constitutional Democrats." In American politics, *constitutional* has consistently served as a euphemism for segregation and oligarchy.

Given that Constitution-worship is, on the whole, a regressive force in political life, it is not such a bad thing that the story of Canada's first constitution is such a poor basis for a cult. It is situated in the recent past, the historical past—not the legendary past. And taken simply as

---

* I know that there are exceptions to this claim and radicals who believed that the Constitution could equally well be enlisted in their cause. Frederick Douglass, for instance, famously called the pre–Civil War Constitution a "glorious liberty document." But while this was powerful propaganda, Douglass's theory that the existing Constitution was antislavery, if rightly interpreted, never received a proper test: slavery was abolished through an explicit new amendment, not through a new interpretation of the existing document. More to the point, the path to that new amendment was paved only by the breakdown of the constitutional order into civil war.

an abstract template for a story, it is singularly unsuited to legend. What kind of legend ends with its heroes asking permission—officially, "Royal Assent"—to succeed in their quest? What kind of heroes conclude their journey by triumphantly asking for a little help from their mother (country)?

To speak again in the rough sense in which myths operate: if American independence was secured in defiance of the British Empire, Canadian independence was secured in fear of an empire. Or rather, in fear of two: the filial and ceremonial fear expressed towards the established British Empire, and the hard, geopolitical fear of the emerging American empire.

Confederation was shadowed by annexation (or worse), threats that the War of 1812 had hardly put to rest. In 1862, the capture of a British ship by the Union army—and the desire of some politicians to use a war with Britain to draw the southern public back into the Union—provoked a minor crisis. London "ordered an urgent deployment of fourteen thousand additional troops to British North America, the largest troop movement there since the War of 1812," before choosing to deescalate. Two years later, amidst fears that the victorious Union army would march north, a British military engineer released a report on the defenses of British North America. Its bombshell conclusion: in the event of an invasion, nothing west of Montreal could be held. Later that year, the Province of Canada's refusal to extradite an arrested Confederate war party set off another minor crisis.

All the participants in Confederation understood how wars shed sparks on kindling well beyond their initial radius. They understood that a newly consolidated, newly powerful American state would be in a mood to expand (as indeed it was, though the expansion ultimately pointed west, to the Great Plains, instead of north). Étienne-Paschal Taché, a veteran of 1812, said that if Confederation failed, "we would be forced into the American Union by violence, and if not by violence, would be placed upon an inclined plane which would carry us there insensibly." Thomas D'Arcy McGee, who fled colonial rule in Ireland, spoke of the geopolitical forces driving Confederation: "Events stronger than advocacy, events stronger than men." These were certainly not impartial assessments—but the fact that some of the leading figures in Canadian politics believed that they would be persuasive does tell us something important about the political atmosphere in which Confederation took place.

Chief among the "events stronger than advocacy" was the British decision to back down from great-power conflict in North America. Canadian self-government is the result of that retreat. Confederation, without the retreat, would not have held off invasion or coerced annexation (though voluntary annexation into a country that had just suffered a ruinous civil war looked increasingly unlikely). No amount of reorganizing the provinces would change the brute fact that they could be defended only at tremendous cost to the British Empire, or the other brute fact that Britain saw little point in paying that cost when the other parts of the empire offered much more lucrative opportunities for plunder, or the final brute fact that the provinces themselves lacked the resources to make up the difference.

Pitched as a nation-building project, Confederation was also a quiet acknowledgment that the new nation would remain permanently undefended, or at least under-defended, against its only conceivable adversary. Its security would lie in the assumption—prescient and accurate, if difficult to publicize—that removing the tinder for great-power conflict, by removing the great power, would effectively secure the peace. The historian Christopher Moore puts the founding calculation in these terms: "If the federated provinces began running their own affairs as a small, peaceable, and trade-minded new nation, while at the same time Britain withdrew its own forces and garrisons and disclaimed all future territorial interests and ambitions in North America, the United States might well come to accept that there was nothing on its northern borders worth a war." And so it did.

Confederation was an explicit agreement among the provinces and with the British Crown—but it was also a tacit agreement with the United States. Canada's geopolitical identity, as no more than a middle power, is as much an unwritten part of its constitution as the principle of responsible government or the office of prime minister. Even the name with which it came into the world—the "Dominion" rather than the "Kingdom" of Canada—was invented out of deference to Americans' republican sentiments.

How could the political culture of the "new Nationality" not be shaped by the compromised and compromising way it came into being? Earlier, I discussed the republican ideal of freedom that animated many of the American founders: the conviction that to be subject to someone else's arbitrary power is to live in a state of unfreedom, or domination. If America was founded on the doubtful pursuit of that ideal, Canada was founded on its impossibility. Since Confederation, Canada, with respect to the United States, has lived in a permanent state of domination—has in fact entered into that state as a condition for its formal autonomy.

We should be precise about what this means. It does not mean that Canada is an oppressed or victimized place. It does not mean that Canada lives under any kind of imminent threat. It is not that America has any rational reason to abrogate the tacit agreement that has functioned well for more than a century and a half. It is simply that it *could*. Long ago, Roman jurists had a legal term to capture that condition: *obnoxius*. It was used "to describe the predicament of anyone who depends on the will—or, as we say, on the goodwill—of someone else." In those days, there was a slave named Publilius Syrus who was granted his freedom and went on to become a famous poet. Looking backwards, he wrote, "The height of misery is to live at another's will."

Perhaps that overstates things. Perhaps, and more to the point, the many varieties of interpersonal domination are questionable models for political domination. Nevertheless, Confederation established a lasting political fact about the new country of Canada: it lives at another's will. How Canadians come to terms with that fact shapes not only our relationship with our neighbour (in the usual euphemism for our hegemon), but also our relationship with our own past.

How do we relate to the few dozen men who put us at another's will—even if (as the many accomplished lawyers among their number would surely point out) there was no realistic alternative? At the extreme, rotten tomatoes and vandalism. And even if those defacements (fictional and real) are aimed at the crime of colonialism, it matters that they are by and large unopposed. There is simply no constituency for Canadian founder-worship, or even founder-appreciation, in the American style. The very best emotions that Macdonald et al. can command—grudging respect for their hardheaded realism, admiration for their eye for a useful compromise—are well short of the emotions that send some two million people to gape at Mount Rushmore each year.

Again, this is not such a bad thing. It is not a coincidence that Canada has, for most of its history, produced politicians of limited charisma: there is only a limited tradition of political charisma on which they can draw. In more optimistic times, that fact made our politics seem devoid of inspiration and energy, almost as insular and closed off as the oligarchical world that the reformers of the 1840s sought to displace. In these times, however, that dispiriting fact looks more like a guardrail—and the brief period between 2015 and 2019 looks like a recent outlier, an experiment in prime ministerial charisma that fortunately failed. The charismatic authoritarianism that lurks in so many democracies lurks at least a little further in the background here. "I alone can fix it" does not exactly translate in Canada.

Nor is it a coincidence that revolution, charisma, and conspiracy theories tend to go hand in hand. The age of revolutions was a great age of imagined conspiracy: How better to explain the maddeningly persistent triumphs of evil, shadowy interests in the face of a supposedly unified popular will? What can bring down a hero other than a stab in the back? From the sinister Jesuits of the eighteenth century to the Trumpian "deep state," conspiracies have done vital political work, explaining why politics, for all the revolutionary, transformative promises, stubbornly goes on being politics. But politics that proceeds on a different mental model—the model that rejects the revolution—is arguably more content to go on being its somewhat drabber self, and thus less in need of excuses for ambiguity, compromise, and disappointment. From this perspective, the conspiracy theories that have emerged as a driving force on the Canadian right—vaccine conspiracies, UN conspiracies, bank conspiracies—are a powerful set of warnings, each of them paving the way for a slashing, strident politics, each of them justifying the coming failures of that politics well in advance.

Above all, the quality that sets off the American political culture from the Canadian is what I would call belatedness: the permanent sense of being too late. It is not just the chasm that separates Americans from their founders; it is that the truly pivotal things, for good or for evil, were done long ago. In the 1838 speech in which a young Abraham Lincoln called for a "political religion" of the founding, he also acknowledged the psychological burdens of worship: to worship is to admit your inferiority.

Lincoln imagined the reaction of a "towering genius," a glory-seeking drive on the level of Washington's
or Napoléon's, on discovering that "this field of glory is
harvested." That genius would inevitably set out to make
a revolution of its own in a land where the revolution
had already happened: "It sees *no distinction* in adding
story to story, upon the monuments of fame, erected to
the memory of others. It *denies* that it is glory enough to
serve under any chief. It *scorns* to tread in the footsteps of
any predecessor, however illustrious. It thirsts and burns
for distinction; and, if possible, it will have it, whether
at the expense of emancipating slaves, or enslaving freemen."

Those lines have been read, understandably, as a
self-portrait: here is the twenty-nine-year-old Lincoln
telling us just how he planned to establish himself as a
new founder, a quarter century before he in fact did so —
just as he predicted, by emancipating slaves. I know of
no better explanation, in such a few lines, of how a successful revolution creates a powerful gravitational field,
pulling subsequent politics back towards its centre — of
how that field can produce both renewed heroism, and
extremities of evil ("enslaving freemen").

And yet, read strictly as a political prediction, Lincoln's words are not quite right: whatever we might say
about the forces upending American democracy, describing them as forces of "towering genius" does not hit the
mark. Perhaps Lincoln erred here because he was a genius himself, and he forgot how resentment and inferiority can trouble souls of even ordinary size. Souls of even

ordinary size, or smaller, can exult in breaking what they cannot build.

In that respect, the most foreboding part of Lincoln's speech is not the passage on the disruptive, amoral genius, who would choose whichever of freedom or slavery won him more glory, but the "happy ending," in which he imagines the threat foiled: "That we remained free to the last; that we revered his name to the last; that, during his long sleep, we permitted no hostile foot to pass over or desecrate his resting place; shall be that which to learn the last trump shall awaken our WASHINGTON."

The happy ending is the return of the dead. The only answer to belatedness is to wait—wait for our fathers to climb out of their graves, wait for the last judgment that will finally make them our contemporaries—and to try to not become deranged in the waiting. I prefer the tomatoes.

———

There is one more way in which Canadian politics is free from belatedness: the modern architecture of its parliamentary system. Of course, *parliamentary* and *modern* aren't supposed to go together. The American Constitution may have been a deliberate construct of Enlightenment reason, but parliaments are supposed to be Gothic accretions of habit that have been piling up since the Middle Ages. Certainly, the visual language of parliamentarism is premodern, from the Usher of the Black Rod to the Speech from the Throne (though Canada fortunately scrapped the British tradition of making the speaker of the upper house sit on a literal sack full of wool). But the political structure of parliamentarism is very much a modern creation.

For one, modern parliaments are only superficially identical to the earlier bodies that bore the same name. They have been transformed by a host of innovations that, together, made them the nucleus of a new form of government. Four such innovations stand out as especially important: parliamentary parties; the transformation of parliamentary parties into mass-membership organizations; ministers' responsibility to parliament; and parliament's accountability to a growing swath of the middle-class, and ultimately working-class, public. Aside from the first, these innovations were all solidified in the nineteenth century; strictly in a chronological sense, modern parliamentarism is newer than the American Constitution.

When the authors of the first Canadian constitution agreed that their country would be governed on the parliamentary model, they were not acting out of a sense of nostalgia or proceeding on colonial autopilot: they were choosing that essentially transformed British system. In their lifetimes, that system had gone through a major period of remodeling, pressured and prodded into some measure of reform by a mobilized working class. And it had enacted two major and highly controversial expansions of voting rights through the Reform Acts of 1832 and 1867. The Fathers of Confederation were not opting into an old and static model, but rather a system that had proved capable of remaking itself. And by choosing a written rather than an unwritten constitution, and a federal rather than a unitary system, they made some important additional changes of their own.

Why does it matter that modern parliamentarism is chronologically newer than the American system? Because some questions about how to organize a large, modern polity, which were genuinely open in 1789, were increasingly closed in 1867, and are even more closed today. In 1789, presidential systems were new and untried—it might really have been the case that creating separate executive and legislative power centres was the key to a stable republic, just as the thought that the planets orbited in circles rather than ellipses once seemed perfectly intuitive. It was not. By 1867, Canadian politicians had accumulated several generations of evidence on the performance of presidential systems: it was cited by Macdonald and others in the Quebec City negotiations, and it did nothing to shake the parliamentary consensus.

With another century and a half of evidence in the books, that consensus is even stronger. Parliamentary systems are more responsive to voters—that is, more democratic. They are far less prone to the constitutional crises that are essentially (if inadvertently) engineered into presidential systems, which give presidents and legislatures dueling mandates from the voters and no clear way of resolving serious conflicts within the bounds of the law. Coups and dictatorships ought to be bugs in the presidential system—but across presidential systems globally, they take place so reliably that they might as

well be features. In a famous paper, the Spanish political scientist Juan Linz found that only two countries,
Chile and the United States, had "managed a century and
a half of relatively undisturbed constitutional continuity under presidential government." But Chile, as Linz
pointed out, had still suffered a right-wing coup in 1973;
and the United States narrowly escaped its own coup in
2021. Even American foreign policy is a tribute to parliamentarism. When Americans restructure foreign governments after war—as in Germany, Japan, and, more
recently, Iraq—they do not import the American constitution. They set up parliaments—an unspoken testament
to the instability of presidential systems.

And yet—conflicting mandates, ministerial responsibility, legislative-executive fusion: none of these seminar-
room terms touch the deep and complicated places where
political emotions live and political cultures take shape.
Institutions, for the really committed localist, are almost
always of secondary importance; they might serve as
symbols of peoplehood or nationhood or some important ideal, but who has ever imagined themselves living, or
dying, for legislative-executive fusion? George Grant, a
father of modern Canadian nationalism, certainly did not
put stock in parliamentarism as a key to Canadian distinctiveness. "Our parliamentary and judicial institutions
may be preferable to the American system, but there is
no deep division of principle," he wrote. "Certainly none
of the differences between the two sets of institutions are
sufficiently important to provide the basis for an alternative culture on the northern half of the continent."

But I think he was simply wrong about that. Parliamentarism *is* a matter of principle, not simply of functionality. There *are* deep parliamentary principles; they have been important to Canadian distinctiveness; and they are seriously threatened in the Canadian present.

First, parliamentarism developed a distinctive and wise response to political charisma: to place it as far away from power as possible. Traditionally, parliamentary systems have found this source of powerless charisma in a constitutional monarch. The idea of impotent charisma emerged almost accidentally, through political struggles between parliaments and monarchs who held very real power. But as those struggles tipped decisively away from monarchical power, many parliamentarians came to see the virtues of retaining a crowned head to serve as a focus for the more atavistic political emotions, and to direct them away from the arena of political conflict. In England, the political writer Jean Louis de Lolme observed that the House of Commons ruled, but that the monarch was covered in "all the personal privileges, all the pomp, all the majesty, of which human dignities are capable." Constitutional monarchy promised the separation of power from pomp—and in backhanded testament to the importance of that separation, dictators and authoritarians have worked to fuse them back together ever since.

At the same time, as the theorist Benjamin Constant observed in France, the crown acted as the "fixed unassailable point" of politics. It would encourage ambitious politicians to play within constitutional rules, including the rule of alternation in power, because ambition's highest reward was permanently inaccessible—literally unattainable on the basis of talent, merit, or popularity. (Francisco Goya's famous portrait of Charles IV of Spain and his family as bejeweled mediocrities—memorably described by a critic as a "picture of the corner grocer who has just won the lottery"—is a perfect portrayal of this ideal. Constitutional monarchs are *supposed* to be mediocrities.) But the theorists of constitutional monarchy also assumed that the somewhat mortifying emotions with which we respond to political charisma or glamour had to be acknowledged and contained. If they were shut up in the body of the sovereign, like nuclear waste, they might not contaminate ordinary politics.

The principled republican response to such ideas has been that those emotions do not need to be accommodated at all, because they are degrading and unworthy of a free people. That itself is a powerful counterideal, and there have certainly been republics where it has been lived out for a time. In the United States, however, the result has mainly been another return of the repressed: a party leader whose own personal fanfare plays when he enters a room. (In France, another presidential-monarchical system, President Macron has welcomed comparisons to Jupiter, the king of the gods.) Symbolism isn't everything in politics, but our choice of symbols often communicates information we would rather not express in words. When prime ministers speak to legislatures, they speak from the floor, in the position of first among equals. Presidents, as any viewer can observe from the American speech from the throne (also referred to by local custom as the "State of the Union address"), literally speak down to legislatures.

The second parliamentary principle I want to point out has to do with that very idea of speaking. Parliamentarism was literally conceived as *government by discussion*—"talk" is in the roots of the word itself. The idea here is not simply that government policy is discussed—something that happens even in the inner circles of dictators—but that discussion itself *is* the government. Power ultimately rests not with the prime minister and the cabinet, but with the public debating body to which they are accountable. In a true government by discussion, no policy is enacted, and no leaders are kept in office, that cannot survive an open, transparent, and adversarial debate. In such a government, the powerful do not simply act—they have to give and defend reasons for everything they do.

Of course, legislative debates happen in presidential systems, too. But the stakes of those debates are generally much lower, as observers of both systems have pointed out since the nineteenth century. In the American system, public deliberations cannot bring about any of the great events in politics: they cannot bring down governments, remove presidents (except under extraordinary conditions that have never been met), or provoke new elections. It would be fair to say that power is less deliberative in presidential systems—and only a bit of a stretch to claim that the political culture produced by those systems is itself less deliberative, because the opportunities for following and vicariously engaging in consequential debates are fewer and farther between. A nation governed by a parliament, wrote the Victorian journalist Walter Bagehot, "is forced to hear two sides— all the sides, perhaps, of that which most concerns it." But under a presidential system, "the prize of power is not in the gift of the legislature. . . . The executive, the great centre of power and place, sticks irremovable; you cannot change it in any event." In a presidential system, the "teaching apparatus" of meaningful debate, "which has educated our public mind, which prepares our resolutions, which shapes our opinions, does not exist."

Perhaps Bagehot was exaggerating his case (the phrase "teaching apparatus," in particular, smells like cod-liver oil), but I think his central point is a sound one: political institutions can shape cultures. Alternative institutions can make alternative cultures.* Parliaments can show us how to argue, why to argue, and whom to argue with.

---

* Two examples: First, by institutionalizing an official opposition to the government, parliamentary systems give visible testament to the fact that disagreement is a permanent, and perfectly acceptable, part of political life. Second, when it is not clear how long a given government can hold on to power, election seasons tend to be much shorter, in part because it is harder to plan them in advance. Contrast this with the regularly scheduled American presidential campaigns, which stretch over nearly two years. Here again, I think there's much to prefer about a system that helps us treat elections as focused arguments for the purpose of resolving an impasse, rather than a system in which parties are forced to invent arguments by the dictates of the calendar. In 2021, Justin Trudeau struggled to point to any such impasse to justify an early election, and Canadian voters denied him a majority—reinforcing the parliamentary norm that early elections need to be called for a clear reason. In American politics, by contrast, the question "Why are we having this election?" never comes up. In its place is a mechanical and routine deference to the calendar—a deference that is at odds with real self-government.

They *can*, but in contemporary parliamentary countries, including Canada, it would be hard to claim that they *do*. Debates on Parliament Hill are now every bit the pseudoevents as the ones that Bagehot yawned at in Congress. They barely make anything happen. They barely have the capacity for surprise. And so, unsurprisingly, they are generally ignored. Government by discussion is a powerful ideal—far more powerful, to my mind, than any ideals produced by presidential politics—but would anyone seriously argue that it currently applies to parliamentary politics in Canada?

On the other hand: Is anyone seriously pining for the return of full-dress, Victorian government by discussion? The very fact from which it derived "its magnitude and its melodrama," in Bagehot's words—the fact that any given debate could potentially change enough representative minds to topple a government—depended on an important and intolerable limitation of democracy. It relied on members of parliament who were, by modern standards, unaccountable to the public and to mass parties—and therefore free, by modern standards, to drastically alter their positions without penalty. Their freedom to persuade and be persuaded was also a freedom from public oversight. And as much as we moderns say that we want our representatives to be open-minded, we also generally want them to do what we elected them to do. Those two goals are in conflict, but the latter has generally won out.

The same forces that have weakened government by discussion have also made constitutional monarchy

irrelevant to most Canadians. For the monarchical oxy-
moron of charismatic mediocrity to make sense, enough
of us have to agree to the fiction that charisma is heritable. For constitutional monarchy to check political ambition or contain political passions, the sovereign really
has to occupy "the most elevated position in society,"
really has to sit at the visible top of the social pyramid.
That is a nearly impossible ideal to maintain in a society
that takes democracy seriously, and in a country whose
monarch lives on the other side of an ocean. If Queen
Elizabeth was able to preserve at least a glimmer of the
old authority, it was as a result of her personal qualities
(especially her prodigiously long tenure) rather than
those of the Crown itself—precisely the qualities that are
not heritable.

I suspect that that is bad news for King Charles; but
it is not very good news for Canada, either. Historically,
Canada's multinational stability owes not a little to monarchy. The idea of multiple nations sharing a single crown,
in contrast to the republican idea of one nation for one
sovereign people, was already centuries old when it was
first put into practice here.* Nor is this ancient history: it
is still vitally important, for instance, to the Indigenous

---

* I understand that, in comparing British and American relations with this
continent's first peoples, we are only parsing various degrees of abysmal.
Nevertheless, at the time of the American Revolution, it was widely understood that the revolutionaries were the party of settlement and dispos-
session. High on the list of grievances in the Declaration of Independence
is the Crown's policy preventing "new Appropriations of Lands"—that is,
the treaties restricting the western expansion of white settlement on native
territory.

nations that stress the fact that their treaty partner is the Crown, not the Canadian government.

———

In sum, the guiding principles that have made parliamentarism the most stable form of democratic government yet invented are difficult to square perfectly with democracy. But many threats to parliamentary government are far less understandable. Among these, the most troubling is the dramatic centralization of power in the Prime Minister's Office (PMO)—a transfer of power from cabinet and parliament to an unelected bureaucracy. This transfer amounts to an unspoken, unwritten constitutional change. And while the transformation has its pivotal moments and actors—particularly Pierre Trudeau, who made his PMO the largest in the world, nearly quadrupling its size—we should also note that it has been endorsed and carried forwards by prime ministers of both main parties, and that it has been echoed from one parliamentary country to another.

Across the world, parliamentary systems have "presidentialized." Collegial cabinet government has given way to government by PMO: the relationship of equals around the cabinet table, which at its best brought pluralism and meaningful debate into the executive, has given way to the top-down relationship of boss and employees. Government by PMO can never be government by discussion, because the important discussions take place well out of sight, and because meaningful discussion depends on a sense of equality among the participants. In some parliamentary democracies, the rot is even further advanced. In Australia, for instance, Scott Morrison's government conducted a secret and unprecedented concentration of power between 2020 and 2022, as the prime minister took personal control of five separate ministries at the height of the pandemic. A Canadian prime minister could easily attempt something similar, because the prerequisite is already in place: a transpartisan conviction that cabinet government does not represent anything worth sacrificing for.

As two parliamentary principles have eroded—the separation of power from charisma, and government by discussion in both cabinet and parliament—prime ministers and party leaders have filled the gap. They dominate mass media coverage, outshining monarchs, governors-general, and other apolitical heads of state. When they win elections, they claim a personal mandate conferred directly by the voters—witness the electoral rebranding of the federal Liberal Party as "Team Trudeau"—without the mediation of unpredictable parliamentary debate. Under these conditions, parliament still has the advantage of unified and decisive action. But many less democratic forms of government do, too.

The trouble is that undermining parliamentary principles has not really exacted a political price. In 2008, Stephen Harper saw off the opposition parties' attempt to form a coalition government, relying on an essentially Americanized argument: voters, not parliament, elect the prime minister; parliament's power to freely choose its leader is an empty formality. Since 2015, Justin Trudeau has led a government of exceptional centralization and troubling secrecy. By 2022, Pierre Poilievre simply assumed Canadians' ignorance about their own form of government: he described himself as "running for prime minister," rather than for party leader, and falsely described that year's Liberal-NDP agreement as a formal coalition rather than a more limited confidence-and-supply agreement. I know that by even raising those points of terminology, I'm playing my assigned role in a trite culture war drama—*pedantic, big-city professor imagines real Canadians care about any of this*—but I cannot help myself. These things are worth getting right. Parliamentary government is our heritage, and watching a generation of politicians undo it in exchange for a point or two in the polls feels like watching someone bulldoze a rain forest.

In fact, we are already living with the results of that undoing: secrecy on one hand, and conspiracy theory on the other. Consider the extraordinary secrecy of the hidden orders-in-council—cabinet decrees that are concealed from parliament and voters alike, and that as of 2015 were literally stored in a locked safe—whose regular use was expanded under Stephen Harper, and expanded even more dramatically under Justin Trudeau. Consider the rotten secrecy of the PMO's intervention in legal matters from the SNC-Lavalin case (in which Trudeau apparently compromised prosecutorial independence in order to shield the construction giant from overseas bribery charges) to, allegedly, the 2020 Nova Scotia mass-shooting inquiry. Undergirding it all is the routine and ordinary secrecy of undeliberative, centralized power.

The undoing of parliamentary democracy has also coincided with the rise of the conspiracy theory to the dominant style on the Canadian right, from Poilievre ("They've been following you to the pharmacy, to your family visits, even to your beer runs") to Derek Sloan (the World Economic Forum is "actually talking about putting microchips in our bodies and in our heads") to Maxime Bernier ("A FUTURE WORLD GOVERNMENT . . . WILL DESTROY CANADA"). It is not a novel point to observe that these sorts of messages are delivered, without fear of contradiction, to siloed and bunkered audiences, that they grow in the dark like mold, that they couldn't bear even a minute of scrutiny. Yet they are a baroque and unreal projection of the very real fact that meaningful politics is conducted far out of ordinary earshot.

The Canadian form of government is, at least nominally, an outstanding defense against just this kind of pernicious nonsense, because it is supposed to do the essential work of proposition and opposition in public. The best alternative to government by conspiracy, and to government by conspiracy theory, is still government by discussion.

But at a certain point, all these dispiriting facts—the banality of debate, the tendency of parliament and cabinet to shrink into rubber-stamp bodies, a presidential system in all but name—simply become the realities to which we have to shape ourselves, if we can. It is the principles of parliamentary democracy that matter, much more than the particular forms in which they happen to be realized in a given era. Maybe Canadians are losing faith in those principles; but maybe, and more hopefully, they are losing faith in only our current system's capacity to embody them.

Parliamentarism has proven enormously flexible at similar moments of crisis in the past—the moments of crisis, for instance, that ultimately gave us responsible government and the expanded franchise. Why shouldn't we expect similar flexibility at this moment of crisis? Provincial-level experiments in British Columbia and Ontario have already put Canada among the world leaders in the use of citizen assemblies: randomly selected bodies, like juries, that offer ordinary citizens a direct role in debating and making policy. Citizen assemblies might propose or review legislation, allocate budgets, oversee regulatory agencies, or deliberate on constitutional changes. Whichever of these roles they take on, wouldn't citizen assemblies make the principle of government by discussion newly meaningful? Next to the public deliberation of ordinary people, wouldn't populist politicians' claim to embody the people look like a theatrical sham by comparison?

The "classical" system of parliamentary government, celebrated by the likes of Walter Bagehot, was always in some amount of tension with democracy—and I suspect that that tension contributes to our era's declining faith in parliamentarism. But enabling ordinary Canadians to participate directly in government by discussion might offer a way out of this impasse: the possibility of a politics that is both more parliamentary *and* more democratic, a politics that preserves our heritage by transforming it.

Rejecting the revolution means choosing to see ourselves as continuous with our past—including our parliamentary past—rather than severed from it "by an
immense cultural chasm." You might see this as a for-
mula for stasis and staleness, for all the old tropes about
cautious, conservative Canada. But I see it as closer to
the opposite. This is not a god-haunted country. Human
hands made it; human hands—ours—can remake it.

Part II
MATERIAL

Chapter 3

SOLIDARITY

EFFECTIVE AND DURABLE MYTHS ARE not invented or discovered. They are laid down like sediment; the particles that form them are the existing materials of culture, history, and memory. I think that individual human beings can help that process of sedimentation along—as I am trying to help it along here—but only by assembling the materials and hoping they cohere.

What I have tried to assemble here is a plausibly antiauthoritarian myth for Canada. It would offer grounds for a greater sense of Canadian separateness from the United States—at a time when separateness is a safeguard against our neighbour's long-term democratic decline. I've also discussed the very real threats to Canadian democracy: the failures of Indigenous reconciliation; the politics of exclusionary *laïcité*; the secrecy, centralization, and paranoia that erode parliamentary government. But with luck, solidarity, and disciplined mental independence, an antiauthoritarian future is plausible here.

But even *if* I've succeeded in showing that, this myth of Canada is left with a real problem. How does it all hold together? What kind of centripetal force keeps all the parts of a decentred, multinational, unrevolutionary democracy from flying off into space? I know that I've sketched a somewhat despairing picture of the ideas of a single, sovereign people, charismatic politics, and constitution-worship; I've done so because I have experienced, viscerally, the grave damage these ideas have done to the possibility of democracy in the country of my birth. But I've also seen the very real political work they do—how, at their best, they can help to make collective self-rule possible. Without them, how do we make shared decisions? Without them, how can there be a *we* at all?

These have long been some of the thorniest questions in Canadian politics, and in politics anywhere. They do not have a straightforward answer, but it might help to consider how they have been answered elsewhere, even when they have been answered poorly and stingily.

As I write this, 277 bills have been introduced in American state legislatures to ban or restrict the teaching of "divisive concepts" in schools. Such laws, or executive orders with similar aims, have gone into effect in nineteen states. Some of them nebulously target the teaching of "critical race theory" or of the concept of systemic racism; a 2021 Texas law explicitly extends the ban to the 1619 Project, a collection of journalism and historical writing with an associated school curriculum, which stresses the central role of slavery and racial oppression in American history.

These bills, and the well-funded, well-coordinated national campaign behind them, have offered a master class in the art of changing the subject. The summer of 2020 was the summer of the George Floyd protests: the largest demonstrations against racial injustice and police brutality—or in any other cause—in American history. The summer of 2021 was the summer of the "CRT panic": a period in which the focus of American anger was skilfully transferred from the figure of a police officer with his knee on a Black man's neck, and the systems of impunity that brought knee and neck into fatal contact, to the figure of a public schoolteacher instructing "our kids to hate America and hate each other" (in the words of a Republican press release)—that is, from a real figure to an imagined one. The backlash was announced and carried through so openly that it was almost a relief from the smog of plausible deniability in which most political malefactors go about their work. "'Critical race theory' is the perfect villain," wrote Christopher Rufo, who coordinated much of the effort from conservative think tanks, in an on-the-record email to a journalist. "Strung together, the phrase 'critical race theory' connotes hostile, academic, divisive, race-obsessed, poisonous, elitist, anti-American." The political calculations were public and unabashed: "The goal," Rufo tweeted, "is to have the public read something crazy in the newspaper and immediately think 'critical race theory.'"

All of which is to say that these people do not deserve the benefit of the doubt. In fact, they have willingly opted out of it. But sometimes, it can still be helpful to extend the benefit of the doubt where it is *not* warranted—to extend it for our own benefit rather than theirs. That's what I would like to do here: to imagine the best possible reason for wanting to ban "divisive concepts" from classrooms, not because I believe that anyone of consequence sincerely holds such a view, but because imagining it can tell us something important about when, and why, divisiveness matters.

As the protests and civil unrest following Floyd's murder entered their second month, a group of Republican senators (the same ones who issued the press release I just quoted) introduced a bill to ban the use of federal funds for the teaching of the 1619 Project—a step that set the tone and messaging for much of the backlash that followed. The bill, as the usual format dictates, included a number of preambulatory statements, or "findings." Here are the last two:

> (5) The 1619 Project is a racially divisive and revisionist account of history that threatens the integrity of the Union by denying the true principles on which it was founded.
>
> (6) The Federal Government has a strong interest in promoting an accurate account of the Nation's history through public schools and forming young people into knowledgeable and patriotic citizens.

What those statements tell me is that the enemies of the sort of public history the 1619 Project represents—

illiberal as they are, full of bad faith as they are—really do understand something about its political stakes. It really does "threaten the integrity of the Union." It really does make social cohesion and solidarity harder to imagine. Myths are coordination points. They do not have to be good or just or fair to coordinate us; even in the absence of those conditions, they can keep a kind of cold social peace for quite some time if they are taught and retaught without competition or contradiction, taught and retaught as "the true principles" of history. The bill's authors aren't wrong to see a challenge to those principles (the principles of the unambiguously virtuous American founding) as a threat, a thaw, to that cold social peace—a threat that was glimpsed, however briefly, in the 2020 riots. We might imagine the bill's authors as engaging in a kind of bloodless realpolitik, not in any direct reckoning with history. Their history may or may not be true, but that is not their most pressing concern. "The Federal Government has a strong interest" in legislating its truthfulness.

That, at least, is what we might imagine if we gave them the benefit of the doubt. And yet, if we do so—if we assume there is some genuine public spirit in these Republicans' feelings for social cohesion—then we are led to ask: Why is received history so important to America's social cohesion in the first place? Why is "divisive and revisionist" history such a threat?

We could answer that question with another question: Besides received history, what else is there to keep the peace? When public schools are effectively segregated, when public spaces are shadowed by random gun violence, when union membership (despite some recent high-profile success stories) remains in a generations-long decline, when wealth and income inequality surpass that of the Gilded Age, when the undemocratic Constitution puts meaningful political power out of reach—when the concrete and tactile bases of solidarity have been so methodically eroded—the only basis of solidarity left is story. Received history bears all that tremendous weight. Under these conditions, it is the only thing that conceivably can. The United States is hardly the only country in which those conditions prevail—but the great weight placed on received history in American politics is an index of the failure of other, material kinds of social cohesion in American life. That cohesion was not destroyed by raving demagogues or insurrectionists. It was destroyed by generations of "normal" politics.

Of course, many of the same politicians who have done so much to erode material solidarity in America—who have undermined the public schools, who have fought union organizing and universal health care with tooth and nail—are the most intent on enforcing the solidarity of received history, by codifying it into law. They are conservatives—and like most conservatives, their thinking grows out of a tradition that places a great weight on social order and social peace. They do not need to consciously accept responsibility for the damage done to those values to accept that damage has been done, by someone or something. So perhaps (again, extending an unwarranted benefit of the doubt) they are trying to undo the damage, to shore up the broken foundation, with the only tools their way of thinking permits them to handle.

Or maybe it is simply the case that material solidarity—the sort of bonds built by reliable public services or democracy in the workplace—is *expensive* from the perspective of capital. And maybe it is the case that immaterial solidarity—the sort of bonds built by enforcing a received history—is cheaper, so that the shift from the former to the latter is nothing more than a cost-saving measure.

Immaterial solidarity does in fact have a "price point"; it can objectively be weighed in the balance with, say, a higher prevailing wage or a shorter workweek. That is one of the most important insights developed by W. E. B. Du Bois in *Black Reconstruction*: his concept of the "psychological wage" is something of a skeleton key to American politics, and to right-populist politics more generally. The psychological wage was pioneered by the planter class and its successors in the American South, and later taken up by capitalists across multiracial America, all of whom converged by trial and error on a remarkable discovery: white workers would accept lower pay and worse material conditions if they were also compensated with a publicly honoured place at the top of the racial hierarchy.

Human beings crave honour; but the tokens of honour—in this case, seats at the front of the bus, exclusive access to drinking fountains or pools, a degree of legal impunity for crimes committed across the colour line, membership in the Real People—are fairly cheap in the scheme of things. They are, after all, *tokens*, status symbols whose worth lies in their exclusivity rather than their intrinsic value. The psychological wage depressed the material wage not through any conscious trade-off, but by sowing enmity and resentment between white and Black workers, limiting possibilities for unified action, and weakening the bargaining position of both groups. For white workers, the psychological wage meant an elite status that not even poverty could compromise; for their bosses, the psychological wage meant a degree of labour peace. Their strategy, wrote Du Bois, "drove such a wedge between the white and black workers that there probably are not today in the world two groups of workers with practically identical interests who hate and fear each other so deeply and persistently and who are kept so far apart that neither sees anything of common interest."

On the steps of the Alabama state capitol in 1965, Martin Luther King Jr. expressed the same idea with a prophetic intensity, speaking of the poor white man who had been taught to "eat" Jim Crow: "When his under-nourished children cried out for the necessities that his low wages could not provide, he showed them the Jim Crow signs on the buses and in the stores, on the streets and in the public buildings. And his children, too, learned to feed upon Jim Crow, their last outpost of psychological oblivion."

The tokens of honour are no longer so explicit—but to this day, the white working class is the pivotal bloc in the right-wing coalition, the group that Trump won by twenty-nine points in 2016 and twenty-six points in

2020.* Those workers are *not* voting against their interests, as the facile liberal line has it. Interest is a complex and nebulous thing, not an entry in a spreadsheet. And if we grasp that, we can also understand how different kinds of interest, and different kinds of solidarity, can be traded off against one another.

The psychological wage, and the movement against "divisive concepts," serve different purposes and grew out of different historical moments, but they are both founded on the same calculation: social peace can be secured by material or immaterial means—with wages and social services, or with stories and tokens—and the immaterial means usually cost less.

It is for just that reason that Canada's marked lack of the usual unifiers—a singular national identity, a Real People, a tradition of charismatic leadership, a revolutionary founding—is so important on a concrete, material level. On the one hand, disunity will always be a (maybe *the*) Canadian problem. The enduring possibility of an independent or quasi-independent Quebec, the alienation of the western provinces, the struggle between

---

* In a striking 1981 interview, Lee Atwater (a political aide to Ronald Reagan and later campaign manager for George H. W. Bush) explained something of how this process works—that is, how even ostensibly race-neutral policies on economics and education can send powerful messages about racial status: "You start out in 1954 by saying, 'n— —, n— —, n— —.' By 1968 you can't say 'n— —'—that hurts you. Backfires. So you say stuff like forced busing, states' rights and all that stuff. You're getting so abstract now [that] you're talking about cutting taxes, and all these things you're talking about are totally economic things and a by-product of them is [that] blacks get hurt worse than whites."

Indigenous nationalists and the Canadian state—these are all as perennial as political questions get. But on the other hand, Canadian disunity means that it is much harder here to substitute the cheap solidarity of story for the costly solidarity of public goods. The harder it is to keep the social peace through a shared, received history—the kind of history the Senate Republicans deemed vital to "the integrity of the Union"—the more it has to be kept by material means, by the constellation of policies that are often called the "social safety net."

For someone who, like me, prefers wages and social services to stories and tokens, this is another reason that Canada's disunity is of such value. And this is one more reason why the processes I described in Part I—the emptying out of the Real People, and the rejection of heroic charisma—matter for Canadians in a very tangible sense. To some extent, we have already been through the worst that the enemies of the 1619 Project and CRT claim to fear: the displacement of our founders from their historical pedestal, the retreat from a history told as a straightforward story of "integrity" (in the sense of either oneness or goodness). These were, as I wrote in the first chapter, the main lines of political struggle in the refounding period of the twentieth century. And if the results of that struggle are for now still mostly settled, then whatever mortar binds us together will have to be made of decidedly prosaic stuff. Conversely, policies like universal health care and parental leave are not simply about health or children: they are part of the material infrastructure that makes it possible for us to reckon honestly and thoughtfully with our past. In fact, universal health care, the centrepiece of the Canadian welfare state, was debated and enacted as the twentieth-century reckoning over Canadian identity was getting underway. I don't think that's a coincidence. To the extent that such a reckoning produces disunity and social conflict—which it *will* if we are doing it honestly and thoughtfully—the material infrastructure of the social safety net protects us from its worst effects. It frees us to be honest with one another. That is one of the things that a safety net is for.

You'll notice my hedging words in the last paragraph: "to some extent"; "for now"; "mostly." I know the danger of exaggerating our differences, as if Historical Reckoning is a particularly difficult course that Canada has passed and America keeps having to repeat. Canada has its own ways of substituting immaterial recognition for harder and costlier material action, a substitution we participate in, for instance, whenever we recite a scripted land acknowledgment, as if a land acknowledgment could provide clean drinking water on reserves.

My own university's land acknowledgment invokes the Dish with One Spoon, "a treaty between the Anishinaabe, Mississaugas, and Haudenosaunee that bound them to share the territory and protect the land." It concludes: "Subsequent Indigenous Nations and peoples, Europeans and all newcomers have been invited into this treaty in the spirit of peace, friendship and respect." I remember the sense of purpose I felt pasting those words into a PowerPoint for my first class; I remember how it never even occurred to me to learn something about that treaty, its history, or the stories of the people who made it, beyond the few hundred words on the university's website. Shortly after that first class, I read that Hayden King, an Anishinaabe scholar who helped to write our land acknowledgment, had come to express some regrets about it: "I started to see how the territorial acknowledgement could become very superficial and also how it sort of fetishizes these actual tangible, concrete treaties. They're not metaphors—they're real institutions, and for us to write and recite a territorial acknowledgement that sort of obscures that fact, I think we do a disservice to that treaty and to those nations."

Acknowledging a treaty is easy; engaging with it as a historical fact that might place some demands on me is, as King suggests, much harder. Harder still is the possibility that it might not take cognizance of me at all—that I might not be automatically "invited" into it. And outside the classroom where I read that land acknowledgment is Toronto, successfully branded as "the most diverse city in the world," where Black people are more than twice as likely to be the target of police "enforcement actions"; outside that classroom is a country in which roughly a third of all the people, and nearly half of the women, incarcerated in federal prisons are Indigenous.

So the phenomenon of cheap solidarity is by no means alien to Canada. But I do think it is less powerful in Canada, for the reasons I have discussed in this book. To the extent that there is such a thing as a Canadian identity, it has to be cobbled together more out of social programs than a shared historical narrative. The health care system, for instance, recurs in surveys and polls as a defining mark of Canadian identity, not necessarily because it is so outstanding (it ranks poorly in comparison with peer countries on measures like cost and access to care) but just for lack of alternatives. It bears some of the weight that the founding bears in American politics.*

But it is not only that these different kinds of solidarity ask different things of us. We experience them in essentially different ways. Compare the anonymous, oceanic feeling of standing for the national anthem in a sports arena with the ability to look your neighbour in the eye as a social equal: someone who can legitimately claim the same social goods as you can, and the same social respect that goes with them. I've experienced both, and again, I prefer the latter—mainly, I think, because it enables me to hold my head up as an individual, because I instinctively resist the kind of dissolution in a crowd

---

* There is an added wrinkle here: no external authority can tell us once and for all what goes in the category of "material" and what goes in the category of "symbolic." That is up to us to sort out as democratic citizens. Take the conflict between Central and Western Canada on climate change and fossil fuel extraction. Is this an argument over emissions targets, carbon taxes, and jobs—or a clash between irreconcilable "ways of life"? If it's the former, then it is amenable to negotiation and compromise; if the latter, then it is a recipe for an intractable culture war. More broadly, Western alienation—the perceived distance of Western Canada from the centres of financial and political power—has served in the past, and might again serve in the future, as a tightly-coiled spring of material change. After all, the origin and spiritual home of our universal health care is Tommy Douglas's Saskatchewan. Few things are more wasteful, from my perspective, than channelling into merely cultural resentment the transformative energy that produced the Co-operative Commonwealth Federation and Medicare. For much of the Canadian right, on the other hand, wasting that energy on culture war is the point.

that the mistier kinds of patriotism seem to require. The solidarity I prefer is small, dense, solid.

In the first, most frightening days of the pandemic—when the snow in Toronto had still not melted; when I let a new purchase from the bookstore sit untouched in the basement for forty-eight hours, just in case; when my hands were raw and cracked from scrubbing—I realized that my American passport was set to expire, and that there would be no way of renewing it any time soon. Even if there had been, travel across the border had come to a virtual halt. I sat every day in an armchair, watching the progress of the buds on the tree outside my window, writing and trying to teach on Zoom, feeling that the decision to immigrate had suddenly and forcibly become irreversible. No passport, closed borders, locked down in a country I barely knew—I know I was letting my fear get the better of me, but it was a fearful time.

One of the things that finally helped to lighten that sense of being trapped was a *Rolling Stone* article that went mildly viral a few months later, when the tree outside the window was full green. It was a polemic by the Canadian anthropologist Wade Davis, explaining America's disastrous COVID numbers as a function of declining social trust, and drawing a contrast with Canada. "On a per capita basis, Canada has suffered half the morbidity and mortality," Davis wrote. "For every person who has died in British Columbia, 44 have perished in

Massachusetts, a state with a comparable population that has reported more COVID cases than all of Canada."*

It was the next bit that made it feel almost a relief to be trapped:

> When American friends ask for an explanation, I encourage them to reflect on the last time they bought groceries at their neighborhood Safeway. In the U.S. there is almost always a racial, economic, cultural, and educational chasm between the consumer and the check-out staff that is difficult if not impossible to bridge. In Canada, the experience is quite different. One interacts if not as peers, certainly as members of a wider community. The reason for this is very simple. The checkout person may not share your level of affluence, but they know that you know that they are getting a living wage because of the unions. And they know that you know that their kids and yours most probably go to the same neighborhood public school. Third, and most essential, they know that you know that if their children get sick, they will get exactly the same level of medical care not only of your children but of those of the prime minister. These three strands woven together become the fabric of Canadian social democracy.

---

* While Davis's figures are from August 2020, the US-Canada disparity in COVID mortality has in fact increased in the years since.

It was, of course, exactly what I needed to hear—
exactly what a certain kind of American liberal, myself
included, wants to believe about Canada. The degree to
which I needed it to be true helped me to overlook the
lovely private school campus not too far down the road;
and the fact that the link between public health policies
and COVID cases turned out to be far less straightforward than it seemed in the early days of the pandemic;
and the fact that, universal health care or no, I cannot
imagine the prime minister's kids spending more than
five minutes in a hospital waiting room; and the fact
that, unions or no, living wage or no, that checkout
person was doing an eight-hour shift on their feet in an
enclosed space in a pandemic while I was sitting in an
armchair looking at foliage. As much as a certain idea
of Canada as a place exempted from the worst harms of
COVID and capitalism helped me through some hard
months, I'm not sure how much it helped that checkout
worker.

And yet, even if there was a degree of wishful thinking
there, it was still wishful thinking of a productive kind—
because Davis expresses so clearly where solidarity comes
from and how it works. It can exist perfectly well without sweeping narratives of national greatness or goodness. It lives in ordinary places: union meetings, doctor's
offices, public schools. It works not only because those
spaces, when they're working well, provide some goods
essential to dignified, comfortable lives, but because they
provide them in full public view. What is essential is not
just that public goods are provided equally, but that they

enable us to *see* other people as equal, and to *be seen* as equal ourselves. "They know that you know": a truce to status-jockeying, the mutual recognition of peers. One does not have to believe that we will be rewarded with an easier plague for living this way to believe that it is an ennobling way to live.

Do we live like that in Canada? I have trouble claiming that we really do: not when union membership has been in decline for my entire life; not when, in August 2022 in my home province of Ontario, an average of 884 people were waiting for an in-patient hospital bed each day; not when 43,000 people left Nova Scotia emergency rooms in 2021 before being treated, "presumably due to interminable wait times"; not when our overcrowded ERs "are full of tension, anger and violence" in the words of one longtime doctor; not when our gap between house prices and incomes is by far the worst in the G7; not when our housing supply is the worst in the G7; not when Toronto and Vancouver regularly top the lists of least affordable cities in the world.

Housing, in particular, puts the lie to our claims to have built a more equitable society. In 1840, LaFontaine wrote that "no privileged caste . . . can exist in Canada," but if he was speaking factually rather than aspirationally, he was simply wrong: the housing crisis has created just such a privileged caste, has given it a financial interest in maintaining the shortage and the political clout to maintain it, and in just a few decades has dramatically expanded the role of inherited wealth in our economy.

But housing is not simply about opportunities to

accumulate wealth, and to speak of it only in terms of wealth—as our politicians generally do—is to trivialize it. A low rent, or a reasonable chance of saving for a down payment, is a reprieve from selling your labour—that is, a reprieve from selling your time.

How much has the cost of housing taken from us collectively? How many deadening jobs and hours-long commutes to afford the rent? How many educations cut off prematurely, how many children never born? Into the sinkhole of housing costs have gone books that were never written, instruments that were never learned, hobbies that were never taken up, start-ups that never made it off the page, dissent that was swallowed in the throat. All these kinds of human flourishing, and many more, need time more than anything else. And so, in a housing market with a ravenous appetite for our time, all these kinds of human flourishing are treated as privileges for the few rather than entitlements for us all.

Yet we *are* entitled to them. Think of the similar entitlement to public space: we set some land off-limits to markets and to private ownership, from national parks to city libraries, so that it can be universally accessible. We certainly fall short of the goal of universal access, but the right to public space is still a powerful concept: it explains why neighbourhoods without green space are dealing not with an inconvenience, but with an injustice; it explains why public access to beaches and forests is as precious an accomplishment (and as fragile) as public education.

Shouldn't we think of public time in the same way?

Like public space, public time is protected from the market, set aside for our free use. It can mean time dedicated to public purposes, like voting, organizing, or volunteering, but it certainly doesn't have to. City parks sometimes host festivals or days of remembrance, but more often host individuals absorbed in their own pursuits: kids' birthday parties and pickup basketball, roller-skating and musical rehearsals, drum circles and endurance runners, teenagers and elderly couples on benches. Just so, public time is largely a matter of individuals trying to flourish as they think best. That thought is captured in the classic labour slogan "eight hours for work, eight hours for sleep, eight hours for what we will." The idea of public time, as the slogan suggests, is hardly a new one: it inspired the movement for the eight-hour workday and the forty-hour workweek, just as it is behind more recent movements for the four-day week or the "right to disconnect." But thinking explicitly about our right to a certain amount of public time helps to clarify the stakes of those movements, and the threat to their goals.

The stakes are human flourishing. The threat is the need to sell our time, and the annexation by the market of the time it takes to flourish. As long as we live in a market economy, we'll be obliged to sell at least some of our time. But just as we intuitively grasp that a city full of well-preserved public space is richer in a meaningful sense, we can also grasp that a country where time is well preserved from the market is also meaningfully richer. And we can understand, as well, how the housing crisis can concentrate wealth in private hands while leaving all of us publicly poorer.

I think that the immediate future of Canadian politics belongs to whoever can speak to economic issues in a language that goes beyond the economic, a language that expresses how something like the cost of housing threatens what we want to believe about ourselves as a country, threatens interests beyond our bank accounts. There is something of that language in Chrystia Freeland's line about the "generational injustice" of the Canadian housing market: "We cannot have a Canada where the rising generation is shut out of the dream of home ownership." But at the same time her line expands the purported injustice to an enormous scale (it is *generational*), it also contracts it to the question of wealth accumulation, leaving aside all the other ways that housing can matter to our flourishing. More prosaically, a governing party whose tenure has been an almost uninterrupted housing bubble will have limited credibility on the issue as long as it stays in power.

By contrast, Pierre Poilievre's video in front of a dilapidated East Vancouver house, blaming the "big-city gatekeepers" for its $4.9 million selling price, has some of the outrage that only an out-party can summon. But, beyond the fact that "big city" is an odd taunt in one of the most urbanized countries on earth, his approach embodies the usual populist strengths and weaknesses. Its strength is its clear target for moral indignation, a target both specific enough for plausibility (in that the ostensible target is the local government and its permitting fees), and vague enough to stand for the nebulous Others, the "gatekeepers," blocking your path. Its weakness is that big, obvious social problems rarely have big, obvious villains. Every current homeowner in Canada (myself included) has at least a narrow kind of self-interest in keeping the housing supply as tight as possible. But our very ordinariness, the ordinary kind of responsibility we bear, makes us poor villains.

A meaningful solution to the housing crisis would almost certainly redistribute economic power along very broad lines, from homeowners to would-be homebuyers, from *rentiers* to renters, from boomers to millennials and to Gen Z. I don't expect a libertarian or classically liberal Conservative like Poilievre to have much interest in that sort of redistribution—or in alienating the relatively comfortable voters whom that sort of redistribution would have to alienate. Hence the need for big, obvious villains.

More broadly, classical liberalism—the philosophy of individualism and the free market—has never been a natural fit for Canadian conservatives. And while that tension is not unique to Poilievre, his leadership campaign brought it to a particularly high pitch, combining as it did the libertarian impulse to make Canada "the freest country in the world" with the flag-waving celebration of the Ottawa blockade as the recent high point of Canadian nationalism (as well as the proximate cause of his political rise). Freedom and nationalism are the twin themes of his campaign's standout phrase (which is also a nod to Wilfrid Laurier, the Liberal prime minister who originated it): "Canada is free and freedom is its nationality."

The trouble with slogans (and I say this having written a few good ones myself) is that the symmetry of their style can mask the contradictions of their substance. More than that, they can make us want to believe that there is no contradiction at all, as if a skillful pattern in words (*nation—free—freedom—nationality*) can persuade our pattern-seeking brains to suspend their skepticism and relax their guard. But in reality, nothing threatens Canadian nationality more than freedom—at least, the limited freedom offered by classical liberals, the freedom of free trade, the minimal state, and the unregulated market.

Freedom, in this sense, has *always* threatened Canadian nationality, which is why the banner moments of Canadian nation-building, for better or worse, have been movements against liberal and market orthodoxy: Macdonald's protectionist National Policy; the state-led settlement of the West; the creation of the CBC/Radio-Canada by a Conservative government, as an explicit barrier against American cultural influence; the building of Hydro-Québec and the signature public works projects of the Quiet Revolution, along with Quebec's antiliberal policies on language and culture, dating back to Bill 101. Nor is the market interested in Indigenous nationality or self-government, except as a hindrance to the extraction of oil or gas. Canadian nationalism—Indigenous, French, and English alike—has meant deliberate resistance to libertarian freedom.

Maybe that has been a historically bad trade: the authors of the 1988 Free Trade Agreement certainly believed so when they made the largest exchange of Canadian nationalism for economic freedom in our lifetimes, and most Canadian voters agreed with them. But at any rate, it has been a *trade*, two separate and contradictory values that have risen and fallen inversely, that cannot be maximized at the same time. I want to be able to make a moral or political evaluation of the freedom-plus-nationalism that is ascending in the Conservative Party—but it can't be evaluated at all. We can only marvel, or shrug, at its incoherence.

In the early Trump years, the political internet rediscovered a 1994 essay by the American military strategist Edward Luttwak, in which he predicted that the contradictions in standard-issue, Anglo-American conservatism would soon run their course. It was a bold claim for the time, just as Newt Gingrich was leading a resurgence of American conservatives; now, in retrospect, it looks almost obvious. "It is only mildly amusing," wrote Luttwak, "that nowadays the standard Republican/Tory after-dinner speech is a two-part affair, in which part one celebrates the virtues of unimpeded competition and dynamic structural change, while part two mourns the decline of the family and community 'values' that were eroded precisely by the forces commended in part one." Luttwak expected the tension to break: and when it did, he expected it to break in the direction of traditional "values" backstopped by an aggressive, interventionist, corporatist state. The title of the essay was "Why Fascism Is the Wave of the Future."

Consider how the tension Luttwak highlights in Anglo-American conservatism applies even more to Canadian conservatism. If market competition undermines traditional family and community values (by encouraging young people to move away from family for work, by pushing both parents to maintain full-time employment, by delegating the care of young children and elders to institutions, and in a host of other ways), how much more does it undermine the identity of a population clinging precariously to a narrow strip on the edge of a market ten times its size? As we've seen, Canadian identity is not very robust to begin with, concentrated as it is in social programs rather than sweeping narratives. If their freedom means weakening and defunding those programs, I expect that Canadian conservatives will find very little nationalism or immaterial solidarity left to work with. I think of a flag hanging limp in a vacuum, like the American flag on the moon, and how it needs to be permanently braced with a hidden crossbar to give the impression of flying. Imagine removing the crossbar.

Of course, none of the incoherence I'm pointing out will harm Canadian conservatives' near-term success in any way. It's a fallacy common to my line of work to think that politicians need to be coherent to be successful. In fact, incoherence can, inadvertently or not, bolster their success: in Luttwak's telling, for instance, fury at eroding social norms generated political power that deregulated markets that eroded social norms, and so on. It works until it doesn't.

Except over the very long run, there is no political

penalty for self-contradiction, a point that applies just as well to, say, Justin Trudeau's pipeline purchase and ban on single-use plastics. And yet—perhaps as a sop to my own professional vanity, perhaps simply as superstition—I insist on believing that a political program cannot really result in deep change to a country's social compact unless it is itself deeply coherent. Coherence is morally neutral: it simply means that all parts of the program, on the level of policy as well as rhetoric, pull in the same direction. Coherent programs, executed over a sufficiently long period of time, can refound countries and challenge the refoundings we believed to be settled. As someone who values Canada's refounding and wants to see it maintained, I'm not so worried about the current iteration of the Conservative Party. I am worried about what's coming next.

What *is* coming next? My best guess starts with a passage like this:

> Never has such a torrent of abuse been poured on any American figure as that during the years from 2016 to 2020. Never have the wealthy and the clever been so united as they were in their joint attack on Mr. Donald J. Trump. It has made life pleasant for the literate classes to know that they were on the winning side. Emancipated journalists were encouraged to express their dislike . . .

and they knew they would be well paid by the powerful for their efforts. Suburban matrons and professors knew that there was an open season on Trump, and that jokes against him at cocktail parties would guarantee the medal of sophistication. . . . Only the rural and small-town people voted for Trump *en masse*, but such people are members of neither the ruling nor the opinion-forming classes.

George Grant wrote that in 1965; I've taken the liberty of changing only the dates and the country in the passage above, as well as the name of the politician to whom it initially applied. John Diefenbaker, the thirteenth prime minister of Canada and the first member of the Progressive Conservatives to lead the government, is not now a well-known figure. But he is the pivotal figure in Grant's *Lament for a Nation*, the populist leader who might have stopped Canada's absorption into the empire of globalized capital, had he not been so thoroughly despised and resisted by the Canadian elite. Personally and politically, Diefenbaker (who began his career as an idealistic criminal defense lawyer on the prairies) had very little in common with Trump—but it is striking to see how little the dynamics of populism, of authentic small-town folk against the globalized elite, have changed in the half century that separates them. It is equally striking that those dynamics are just as native to Canada as to America.

I've mentioned Grant's *Lament* a number of times

already, because it is a foundational text of Canadian nationalism in the modern era—the post–World War II era in which American hegemony emerged as the greatest threat to Canadian independence. Grant is worth grappling with both where he's right (the fact that Canadian elections have not been exempt from the interference of the US national security state), and where I think he's wrong (his claim that the Canadian and American systems of government embody the same values). Above all, his book matters now because it turns out to be darkly prophetic: it foretold the politics that Luttwak saw as a renewed "fascism," and which I'll simply call (sticking to its preferred name for itself) "national conservatism."

Grant was very much a nationalist of the old school, whose vision of Canadian distinctiveness was bound up with the Burkean ideals of tradition, hierarchy, and self-discipline. Canada, for Grant, was mainly a quixotic attempt to live out such ideals while sharing a continent with the most dynamic economy on earth, a machine that eats those values for breakfast. Canada's English settlers were not an ideological or theoretically inclined lot, but they were motivated by "inchoate desire to build, in these cold and forbidding regions, a society with a greater sense of order and restraint than freedom-loving republicanism would allow . . . a society of greater simplicity, formality, and perhaps even innocence than the people to the south." In that desire, many of them, including Grant, had been content to make common cause with the high-Catholic conservatism of prerevolutionary Quebec, and the politics represented by Maurice Duplessis and the Union Nationale.

But what Grant understood—in a way that few contemporary Canadian conservatives do, and still less the flag-waving truckers at the Ottawa "Freedom Convoy" blockade—is that Canadian nationalism would always be at risk from market forces, from classically liberal freedom. Economic logic pointed to deeper and deeper continental integration, to more and more uniformity, and therefore to the erosion of Canada's distinct cultures, both English and French. Canada's elite, as the local spokespeople of global capital, were the instruments of that integration, and they profited handsomely from it.

Grant's conclusion was that Canadian nationalism had to be anticapitalist:

> Capitalism is, after all, a way of life based on the principle that the most important activity is profit-making. That activity led the wealthy in the direction of continentalism. They lost nothing essential to the principle of their lives in losing their country. It is this very fact that has made capitalism the great solvent of all tradition in the modern era. When everything is made relative to profit-making, all traditions of virtue are dissolved, including that aspect of virtue known as love of country. This is why liberalism is the perfect ideology for capitalism. It demolishes those taboos that restrain expansion. Even the finest talk about internationalism opens markets for the powerful.

In fact, the only way of conserving Canadian identity, and Canadian "innocence," was economic self-sufficiency: insulation from the power of global capital, and American capital in particular. Traditional values could be preserved *only* under a planned, socialist economy: "Nationalism had to go hand in hand with some measure of socialism. Only nationalism could provide the political incentive for planning; only planning could restrain the victory of continentalism." Because Canadian elites were insufficiently patriotic to restrain their profit motive (unlike, Grant argues, their counterparts in Gaullist France or Communist Cuba), and because Diefenbaker's Progressive Conservatives were too feckless to put up a last-ditch opposition, Grant insisted that the virtual annexation of Canada had already taken place. Canada and conservatism were synonymous, and both had lost: "The impossibility of conservatism in our era is the impossibility of Canada."

Strangely enough, Grant won a following on the Canadian left—a group of readers who celebrated Grant's anticapitalism, but forgot to read (or deliberately ignored) the parts about what that anticapitalism was supposed to be *for*. It was supposed to be for the protection of patriarchal, Christian "order"—a vision of Canada as Salazar's Portugal or Franco's Spain. It was as if the combination was so surprising in mid-to-late-twentieth-century North America that one half of it—the pivotal half—simply did not register.

But in an earlier generation—or a later one—Grant's politics would not have seemed unintuitive at all. In my grandparents' generation, right-wing governments from Mussolini onwards regularly co-opted the language of economic planning and socialism; the problem with capitalism was not that it enabled class domination, but that it undermined the traditions and integrity of the nation. (Needless to say, this right-wing anticapitalism was quite often anti-Semitic, as well; Grant's book is mercifully free of that sin.) In my own generation, it is once again increasingly common for conservative parties to array themselves against "big tech" and "woke capital." Their antimarket posture has not resulted in any concrete policy change, at least not yet—they are still happy to give "woke capital" a tax cut—but at the very least, the contradictions of the standard Republican/Tory after-dinner speech are beginning to grow unbearable.

At the inaugural National Conservatism Conference in July 2019, Republican senator Josh Hawley said that "the reigning political consensus shows little interest in our shared way of life." That consensus, he claimed, favours "closer and closer economic union, more immigration, more movement of capital, more trade on whatever terms. The boundaries between America and the rest of the world should fade and eventually vanish." George Grant might have allowed himself a smile of recognition there: the market forces that had long since begun to erode the national identity of small countries like Canada had at last come for the hegemon. When Stephen Harper and Erin O'Toole describe politics as a clash between the rooted "somewheres" and the rootless "anywheres"; when Tucker Carlson celebrates Viktor Orbán's Hungary as the rare country where hard state power has been put in the service of traditional values and anti-immigration; when Orbán himself "confidently declare[s] that Christian democracy is not liberal"—they are all channeling the old insight that Grant himself channeled for Canada: capitalism is the universal solvent.

Think of how Orbán put it, also in July 2019: "In a liberal system, society and nation are nothing but an aggregation of competing individuals. What holds them together is the Constitution and the market economy. There is no nation—or if there is, it is only a political nation. . . . When there is no nation, there is no community and no community interest."

Much of the centre left remains dumbfounded at the idea of a conservative leader saying anything critical at all about the market, or consumerism, or capitalism. For the moment, a neofascist like Italy's Giorgia Meloni—who offers traditional "identity" as the last defense against the market forces producing "perfect consumer slaves"—has the genuine advantage of rhetorical surprise. But in the broad scope of history, this is *the* conservative idea. It descends from Masitre, Bonald, and the other reactionaries who organized the intellectual response to the French Revolution. It is the idea that ruled much of Europe in the 1930s and made serious inroads in North America, that inspired Grant's conservative polemic for a planned economy, and that is once more reasserting itself in our time. The more incoherent kind of conservatism—the kind in which market and family, capital and nation, are squeezed together like opposite magnetic poles—may one day be seen as merely a brief interruption in that history.

It is fair to ask why, or whether, this is a problem in the first place. Libertarian conservatism really did do severe damage to the kinds of solidarity that I value—shouldn't I be excited at the prospect of its displacement? I've said some positive things about localism (Canadian localism in particular) and some critical things about capitalism—shouldn't the people doing the displacing be my allies, or at least the enemies of my enemies?

No—I shouldn't, and they shouldn't. To explain why, it helps to go back to Grant again, and to consider now his key distance from today's national conservatives. Grant wrote before what I've called the Canadian refounding, or in its very early days. He was describing a much more homogenous place than today's Canada (and a place made more homogenous by omission: Grant's Canada has no Indigenous presence to speak of, and he in fact uses the word *indigenous* only to describe the cultures of English and French Canada). Given that fact, there is little room, or need, for ethnic rancor in his politics. His case against Canada's elite is that they have compromised its sovereignty, not that they have deliberately set out to replace the Real People. If Grant had achieved his goal of a self-sufficient, socialist country, it would presumably have been a country in which socialism's public goods were widely available.*

---

* Of course, Grant also made clear from the first page his goal would not be achieved because the cause was already lost. This may be another reason for

The tenor of today's national conservatism is very different. It is not a project to preserve. It is a project to forcibly restore something that is imagined to have been stolen, something that wears various masks—"manhood" for Hawley, rootedness for O'Toole, the Christian community for Orbán—but that generally amounts to the same thing in each case: the powerful sense of an entirely lost social world. As usual, Orbán has made the point with the smallest degree of shame: "This is why we [Europeans] have always fought: we are willing to mix with one another, but we do not want to become peoples of mixed race."

In power, a modern national conservatism may well be more generous with social goods than the conservatism it is aiming to displace. But it will use those social goods for a decidedly illiberal purpose: to limit membership in the Real People, to indicate visibly and publicly who belongs and who does not. Earlier, I wrote about why the publicness of these goods—a space like the public school drop-off, the doctor's waiting room, the union hall—is so important. There is a powerful sense of shared membership and shared interest—of solidarity—that comes from using these goods in the sight of others. National conservatives understand this point intuitively— and they also understand that there is no requirement that social goods belong to everyone. They can just as

---

his following on the left—our affection for conservatives without a political program. In general, we on the left enjoy keeping a handful of conservatives around to sing laments for the lost past. It makes us feel important.

well be used to build bonds of solidary among some at the expense of others. They can just as well be used as tools to rebuild that nebulous, lost thing.

This perversion of socialism to build a hierarchy of belonging is historically common enough that there's a name for it: *herrenvolk* (or "master race") democracy. When national conservatives describe the beneficiaries of the public spending they want, they generally describe a man engaged in the kind of industrial work that our culture imagines as white dominated, not the fields like teaching and nursing in which women and workers of colour play a much larger role. In Hawley's words, "We must make every effort to restore a vibrant manufacturing sector in this country that can employ working men at living wages—wages that can feed a family." In the words of Trump's political strategist Steve Bannon, "I'm the guy pushing a trillion-dollar infrastructure plan. . . . Shipyards, iron works, get them all jacked up. We're just going to throw it up against the wall and see if it sticks. It will be as exciting as the 1930s, greater than the Reagan revolution—conservatives, plus populists, in an economic nationalist movement." In pursuing that program, national conservatives can draw on models from the European far right, like Marine Le Pen, who casts immigration as the essential threat to the welfare state. And they can draw on models much closer to home: the heavy subsidies that made possible the interstate-connected, racially exclusive suburbs of postwar America; the deliberate exclusion of most Black workers from FDR's initial version of Social Security; the well-funded white schools of the segregated South; the state-organized colonization of Western Canada.

Trump's failure to follow those models, and to listen to Bannon's explicit advice urging him to do so, was the single most providential failure of his presidency. As frightened as I am of the angry, failed, coup-fomenting version of Trump, I would have been far more frightened of the Trump who used state power and public spending to build a durable popularity and a lasting political realignment: shipyards *and* the Muslim ban, ironworks *and* the Wall, Trump as the American François Legault. Implausible as that sounds now, recall that Trump won the 2016 Republican primary by running to the left on social spending, promising to preserve Social Security and Medicare, and recall that some of his closest advisors were pushing him in the direction of massive infrastructure spending from the first days of his presidency. Instead, Trump ignored that advice and governed like a conventional Republican (or did not have enough sway over his party to govern otherwise), narrowly failing to repeal Obamacare and passing a regressive tax cut. The passage of that tax cut marked the lowest ebb of approval in Trump's entire presidency, lower even than the aftermath of January 6. The realignment never happened.

We might attribute that missed opportunity to Trump's laziness or lack of discipline, but we could just as well attribute it to some of the structural forces in American politics: the persistence and the deep roots of libertarian conservatism, the powerful donors who fund and advocate for it, the long-standing networks of activists who perpetuate it. As I've said, incoherence is no barrier to success, at least in the short term. So while I believe that the national conservatives are basically correct about the incoherence of their libertarian rivals, and while they have their own, growing network of wealthy funders (including the likes of Peter Thiel), coherence is not enough. So far, they have the power to introduce borrowed terms like *working class*, *multinational corporations*, and *capital* into the Republican vernacular. They do not have the power to govern outside the party orthodoxy—not yet, at least.

But in Canada, the equivalent orthodoxy is far weaker. It is not simply that our more tightly regulated elections place at least some limits on the political power of capital. It is that Canada's political culture and nationalism have been bound up with the interventionist state since Confederation. To a far greater extent than in America, Canada's sense of national belonging has been a creature of the state; the state has been its most effective protector against the entropic forces of continental integration and virtual annexation. I suspect that national conservatism will resonate even more strongly here in the years to come, because it is a very natural (if ultimately cowardly) set of ideas to have on the edge of an empire. To be a national conservative in America is to acknowledge that even the United States, for all its power, is only a very large province in the empire of capital—and I don't think that a critical mass of Americans is ready for that acknowledgment. In Canada, our place on the periphery has never been in doubt.

The interventionist state, which has enabled Canadians to maintain at least something of a distinct political culture on this continent, can also be put to other uses. In a determined set of hands (whether belonging to the current leaders of the federal Conservative Party and its provincial allies, or to the leadership a few trial-and-error iterations down the road), it could reopen a set of questions most of us believed were closed, and it could challenge the Canadian refounding. It will wear a hard hat or drive a truck, it will identify itself with the working class, it will take naturally to Grant's language about paid-off journalists and liberal professors (adding to it only the dark figure of the immigrant with whom they are in cahoots), its Christianity will come in an acceptable variety of flavours (from evangelical to *laïque*), and it will have a growing contingent of allies in America and around the world.

As for those of us who value the refounding, who want to see its rejection of the Real People maintained because we see in that rejection the well-being of Canadian democracy: What can we do in response? Here again, the idea of the psychological wage is helpful. National conservatism promises not just a set of material goods—jobs at shipyards or new highways or more health care spending—but also exclusive access to those goods, the dedication of those goods to the cultural goal of rebuilding the patriarchal family or the Christian nation. Sometimes, even as wealth continues to concentrate itself, the argument will be put in terms of scarcity: "Refugees are the reason your school is crowded, asylum seekers are the reason you can't see the doctor, immigrants are the reason you can't buy a house." But exclusivity, rather than scarcity, will do the vital psychological work. It will offer the high pleasures of belonging, and the belief (not unheard-of among liberal urbanites) that one's consumption serves a higher ethical purpose. It will offer, as well, the low pleasures of living in some proximity to the excluded, and knowing them to be excluded.

What we have to offer in opposition to this—what the left has always had to offer—is essentially a better material deal. The larger the bloc negotiating—not just in the formal bargaining of unions, but in the larger negotiations of politics, from voting to street protests and work stoppages—the more power it can bring to bear, the greater rewards it can secure. The farther we can extend our solidarity, the more we will find our world to be (in a wonderful old word I wish were in greater use) *commodious*: amply furnished with the good things in life, and full of the time and space to enjoy them.

I wish there were something more to say. I wish there were words about our shared humanity or cosmopolitanism that could measure up even a little bit to the power of that vision of the clean, lost world. But there just aren't any. We've known that since at least 1914, when the workers of the world marched off to slaughter one another for God and country, all the best socialist talk about international brotherhood bouncing off of their helmets, drowned out by their marching bands. Nietzsche said somewhere that the powers that be will always have the best arguments: the drumroll and the fanfare. They still do.

And this is one of the reasons why the left, for much of its history, has struggled so mightily. We do not have a better fanfare—just a set of small, dense, solid things. We are materialists. And if there is ultimately something more than the material in our politics, it comes only through the act of seeking those things alongside others. Standing on a picket line with strangers, withholding our labour and forgoing our wages for the sake of our coworkers, recognizing that we share a community of interests even with people with whom we can barely communicate: this is the way to what the great radical thinker Mike Davis called "moral self-recognition through solidarity." This is the way to "structures of feeling that others would deem spiritual."

Those feelings do not live outside the world, but *in* it, in the work alongside others to achieve the most prosaic things: a little more money, a little more time, eight hours for what we will. And so when I read that "Democracy Dies in Darkness," or that "democracy is on the ballot," I don't doubt that slogans like those can mobilize voters and win elections—but I still recoil from them. I recoil because of their fundamental, cloying dishonesty: their patronizing promise that we can skip straight to the "spiritual"—the stirring, heroic defense of big abstract nouns—and pass over the hard things of this world.

Our challenge is protecting democracy without smothering it in reverence: without treating it like a sacred object, a kind of holy relic that goes on procession every two or four years, whose bearing on our lives is not entirely clear and is never explained in much detail, which cannot be examined too closely, but which must be defended at all costs.

Fetishizing democracy tells me nothing about how it will make my life better, fairer, or freer in a concrete sense. Fetishizing democracy helps us to *avoid* talking about those things. It is an easy step—deceptively easy—from the idea that democracy is on the ballot to the idea that democracy is *only* on the ballot: that the unfreedom of the workplace is not really unfreedom, that the dictatorship of the boss is not really dictatorship, that the principle of living together as free and equal people does not apply as long as we are on the clock.

Those who fought to bring democracy into being, who knew its absence, who saw what that absence meant in the hard lives of the people on whose behalf they spoke, were entirely willing to speak of it in the least sentimental terms. They understood that democracy was not an idol, not an icon, but a power: a political power raised up to contend with economic power.

Du Bois understood: "Is it possible, and probable, that nine millions of men can make effective progress in economic lines if they are deprived of political rights?"

Douglass understood: "Let the Negro once understand that he has an organic right to vote, and he will raise up a party in the Southern states among the poor, who will rally with him."

LaFontaine understood: "Without political liberty we have no future; our needs cannot be satisfied."

These are the unabashed terms of need and want, the language of *this* world. Because these democrats cared for democracy, and because they feared for it, they could not afford to worship it; nor can we.

Chapter 4

POWER

MOST EXPERTS WILL TELL YOU that Canada has not released an official review of its national security policy since 2004, but they are forgetting about *Come from Away*. In the absence of a more formal document, the hit musical, which opened on Broadway in 2017, is the defining text of Canada's foreign relations in this era. The true story of the thirty-eight planes and nearly seven thousand passengers diverted to Gander, Newfoundland, after the 9/11 attacks, and of the townspeople who moved heaven and earth to accommodate them, is everything Canada would like to believe about itself, and everything Americans would like to believe about Canada. The perpetual helpful neighbour, the dispenser of winter coats to refugees, the place removed from war and terrorism but very happy to help clean up afterwards. The place (in the words of a poem by Al Purdy quoted in Atwood's *Survival*) "a little adjacent to where the world is."

Why (I'd ask, only half-facetiously) shouldn't that

count as a national security document? National security starts from a sense of who is being secured and what is worth securing, a sense of which interests are dispensable and which are nonnegotiable, an effort to determine which answers to those questions can command a critical mass of support. Those are all things that we hash out through the broad area of human activity that we call culture. There is a reason that rulers of all kinds, from chieftains to prime ministers, have patronized the arts since before the written word existed: because they have intuitively understood, better than many artists, the stakes of culture.

Come from Away attained quasiofficial status in Canada on March 15, 2017, the week after President Trump signed an executive order giving legal form to his campaign promise of "a total and complete shutdown of Muslims entering the United States." On that evening, Justin Trudeau and the Canadian consulate general in New York welcomed six hundred guests (many of them "exuberant Canadians, some bearing flags or wearing clothing decorated with the maple leaf") to a special performance on Broadway. Trudeau took the stage to introduce the musical with a little speech—"There is no relationship quite like the friendship between Canada and the United States. This story, this amazing show, is very much about that, and it's about friendship as well"—and then took his seat in the audience next to Ivanka Trump, presidential daughter and advisor.

Alliances are made out of just these sorts of constructive dishonesties—from the little dishonesty of describing our relationship as a "friendship" (isn't friendship a relation of equals?), to the graver moral dishonesty of sitting next to a Trump in the dark while the show depicts a Muslim passenger humiliated and strip-searched before boarding his return flight. Of course, nothing else was ever a remote possibility. Social media would have exploded if Trudeau had used his remarks to make the obvious connection between art and life, but there is a reason that sort of thing only happens in *Love Actually*. Some righteous moral indignation might have been satisfactory and well deserved—but what would it have actually accomplished?

The answer is probably "less than nothing." But the question can also be turned on its head. What does the anodyne talk about friendship accomplish? What does the parading of Canadian inoffensiveness accomplish? What is accomplished by the elevation into the national myth of one particular moment of Canadian-American comity, before Iraq, before the extraordinary renditions, before Abu Ghraib, before the drone war?

Those are genuinely not rhetorical questions. The powers of this world have to be flattered. There is essentially only one way for a vastly less powerful country to address the hegemon with which it shares an undefended border, and on whom its economy is largely dependent—so the posture of inoffensiveness on its own tells us nothing. "There is no relationship quite like the friendship between Canada and the United States": they *could* be the words of moral cowardice; they could equally well be the sort of shrewd and politic words one uses while trying to wrest a maximal freedom of action from unfavourable conditions.

My concern is not about the self-presentation of the innocent, helpful, neighbourly Canada, but rather about what this self-presentation is supposed to be *for*. My fear is that it is for nothing: that, for the current political class, the posture of inoffensiveness is an end in itself, not part of the determined and self-confident creativity it is going to take to live next to an eroding democracy, without eroding ourselves.

―――――――

In the last chapter, I mentioned the double-edged nature of Canadian-American trade: the source of much of our wealth has also been the source of our dependency. Canadian localism has generally gone hand in hand with resistance to free trade with the United States (and sometimes with a longing for a return to the embrace of the British mother country), as it did at Confederation, in the days of Macdonald's National Policy, in the nationalist resurgence of the late 1960s, or in the ill-fated resistance to the 1988 Free Trade Agreement. Yet geography and economics have put Canadian localists in a difficult-to-impossible position. Either their protectionism was a constrained reaction to American protectionism (as Macdonald's was), in which case their gestures of independence were mainly a matter of sour grapes; or it was a truly voluntary attempt to "buy back the country," in which case it seemed to be an elitist project that would put their fellow citizens out of work in the name of an insubstantial ideal. A few brief reversals aside, our continent's economic integration has ratcheted steadily upwards for generations.

This has led to some odd consequences. One is the embarrassing weight placed on consumer products as markers of Canadian identity. In the words of the satirical news site *The Beaverton*: "Anglo Canadian Culture Revealed Just to Be a Series of Brand Loyalties." The rare objects that seem to have been spared by the unstoppable process of integration take on a totemic heft. Something like a Coffee Crisp bar becomes an uncanny object, mysteriously passed over by the forces of globalization.

But the Coffee Crisp, the ketchup chips, the "I am a Canadian" ads, and the rest are only the tongue-in-cheek aspect of a more serious and more dispiriting idea: on a continent so tightly integrated, *meaningful* independence—separateness of mind, of politics, of culture—is not really possible. Our efforts to imagine ourselves as separate, more often than not, run into a brick wall of economic determinism. We can disagree about the precise date on which the wall became impassable, whether we identify the decisive moment with NAFTA, or the 1988 Free Trade Agreement, or the 1965 Auto Pact, the wartime continentalism of the Mackenzie King government, or even the settlement patterns of Upper Canada. We can protest economic integration from the right (for undermining the family, the church, and other traditional authorities that are more powerful in a poorer country) or from the left (for subjecting us to the dictates of international capital), or we can celebrate it as a force for competition and progress. But all these perspectives share a key premise: that the economy is where the action is, and that Canadian culture and politics are bound to closely track their American counterparts as long as the two economies are so tightly bound together.

This has the advantage of scanning as the hardheaded, realist view. But, as with many kinds of "realism," it turns out to be a kind of wishful thinking. In this case, the wish seems to be that someone or something else, but certainly not us, would take responsibility for what has become of us. The realities of trade and commerce, though, have never exempted societies from the responsibility for making collective decisions about how to live together.

The best recent discussion of this idea that I am aware of comes from the anthropologist David Graeber and the archaeologist David Wengrow. They point out that links of travel and exchange across vast areas—the Pacific Rim, for instance, or the North American river systems—are as ancient as they are modern. Then as now, ideas, practices, and technologies travelled with people. But if "globalization" has deeper roots in human history than we might suspect, then where is the cultural homogeneity that is inevitably supposed to accompany it? "If everyone was broadly aware of what surrounding people were up to . . . then the question becomes not why certain culture traits spread, but why other culture traits didn't. The answer . . . is that this is precisely how cultures define themselves against their neighbours. *Cultures were, effectively, structures of refusal.*"

The practices, objects, and ideas we take from others—and those we decline to take—can be a matter of conscious choice, of deliberate, collective self-fashioning, of making and marking our differences from our neighbours. Historically, they quite often have been. As the twentieth-century anthropologist Marcel Mauss put it, "Societies live by borrowing from each other, but they define themselves rather by the refusal of borrowing than by its acceptance."

Of course, this is an argument drawn from the human past, not the present, with its far more intensive flows of capital, people, and goods. What held in the world of birchbark canoes may not hold in the world of inter-modal shipping containers. But consider the case of Red and Blue America. Their economic integration is nearly total. There is complete freedom of movement between the two. There are no customs checks or passport controls between Texas and California, or between Ohio and New York, let alone between city and exurb in any of those states. And yet, Red and Blue America are increasingly coming to understand themselves as distinct societies—and ultimately, as I proposed in the first chapter, maybe even as the homelands of new ethnicities.

American polarization is wrenching; but from another perspective, it is a reminder of the limits of economic determinism, of the possibilities for freedom and creativity that are open to us even under conditions of economic interdependence. What would it mean to think about Canada's past and future in terms of its "structures of refusal"? What would it mean to think of our history not in terms of the many imported ideas we have accepted, but of the pivotal ones we have rejected? Refusal need not be provincial or small-minded: it can be a kind of self-making, the best defense diversity has against homogeneity.

In fact, some of Canada's most creative periods were periods of refusal. One of the most dynamic forces in our political history has been anti-Americanism. I mean anti-Americanism not as a knee-jerk prejudice or unearned superiority, but as a cold assessment of how American power has often been incompatible with Canadian goals. Confederation, and the emergence of an autonomous and unified Canada, is hard to imagine without the backdrop of the American Civil War and the fear of annexation. The era of the National Policy was a period of protectionism, but also a period of railroad-building and increased integration of the Canadian provinces through east–west trade. In the twentieth century, the Diefenbaker government—"almost a parody of anti-Americanism," in the words of a recent scholar—rolled back racial bias in immigration policy, several years before the United States did the same. That decision, which was explicitly linked to aspirations for greater economic self-sufficiency, laid the groundwork for the transformation of Canada's ethnic makeup. And the period of Canada's refounding also encompassed the Third Option: the 1972 policy developed by Mitchell Sharp, the secretary of state for external affairs, to "reduce the present Canadian vulnerability" to American influence.

The proximate source of this vulnerability, for Sharp

and the Pierre Trudeau government, was the "Nixon shock" of August 1971: the imposition of an import surcharge and the abandonment of the gold standard, policies designed to rectify the American balance of trade with Europe and Japan, with Canada caught in the cross fire. Rarely had the asymmetry of the Canadian-American "friendship" been brought home so conclusively: some 70 percent of Canadian exports went to America, while just 20 percent of American exports flowed in the other direction, a reality that left Canada exposed to unpredictable movements from its dominant trading partner. Rarely had the distance between Canadian and American interests been demonstrated so vividly, a point that no one made better than Nixon himself in a 1972 address to the Canadian Parliament: "It is time for Canadians and Americans to move beyond the sentimental rhetoric of the past. It is time for us to recognize that we have very separate identities; that we have significant differences; and that nobody's interests are furthered when these realities are obscured."*

The most damaging aspects of the policy were soon rolled back, but as Sharp later put it, "the special relationship came to an end" with the Nixon shock. In this case, the term "special relationship" did not refer to a gauzily disproportional sense of friendship, in the way

---

* Imagine being a member of that parliament and being instructed by a visiting head of state to remember that you represent an independent country. That statement, as correct as I believe it to be in the abstract, was surely intended to shame its listeners. Richard Nixon was a shrewd reader of resentments.

that British politicians sometimes use it, but to a specific claim: the Canadian and American economies were so interconnected that America *could* not inflict pain on Canada without also inflicting pain on itself, and therefore *would* not. The Nixon shock showed that that assumption no longer held. But, beyond economics, resentment of American influence had already been building in Canada for some time. These were the years of the Vietnam War and the flight to Canada of American draft dodgers, of political assassinations and civil unrest, of the racial retrenchment that brought Nixon to power in the first place. Then, as now, American power took on a troubling cast for many Canadians, who agitated (in the words of a retrospective) for "far-reaching policies to take back the Canadian economy from its American overlords." Nearly a quarter century after the Third Option paper, Sharp was still forthright about these political goals: "Geography . . . subjects Canadians to a heavy barrage of political and cultural influences. To maintain our identity we have always had to lean against these Americanizing influences."

We cannot understand the Third Option paper without understanding how it was shaped by a wariness of American power in culture and politics—not simply in economics. Perhaps that is also why it read more like a campaign platform than a policy proposal, released as it was just two weeks before the October 1972 election in which Trudeau was narrowly returned to power. But while the paper was notoriously short on concrete detail, and while Sharp later described it as an effort to co-opt and neutralize advocates for "the more extreme kinds of nationalist measures," it did make a compelling case for unwinding the continentalist policies of Trudeau's Liberal predecessors.

As framed by Sharp, that unwinding, as difficult as it would be, was the best of three potential ways forwards. Option one was the status quo, which Nixon had just proved unsustainable, by showing that the United States could unilaterally revise it at any time. Option two was deeper integration and pooled sovereignty on the European model, a model Sharp dismissed as unworkable for a partnership of only two countries with an immense disparity in power. The third option was a program of trade diversification abroad, and industrial policy at home, in order to "lessen the vulnerability of the Canadian economy to external factors, including, in particular, the impact of the United States and, in the process, to strengthen our capacity to advance basic Canadian goals and develop a more confident sense of national identity."

Though the Third Option was taken up as official policy, little came of its plans. A new agency to review foreign investments in Canada was largely toothless. New trade agreements were signed with the European Community and Japan, but these were largely symbolic, and led to little in the way of expanded trade. As much as the government saw a diversified set of trading partners as essential to "basic Canadian goals," the private sector disagreed. By the 1980s, it was clear that the integration of the Canadian and American economies was irresistible. Canada had defaulted to option two, a consensus solidified by the 1988 Free Trade Agreement and Brian Mulroney's trouncing of the nationalist holdouts in the subsequent election.

From a narrowly economic perspective, then, these periods of Canadian anti-Americanism were nothing more than a series of inconsequential blips. While they may have won a handful of politicians some rounds of cheap applause, they meant nothing next to American power and wealth, nothing next to the capitalist logic pushing inexorably towards the most profitable markets and the most efficient exchanges. But it would be wrong to consider the economy in isolation from the rest of Canada's political culture. Trade is not the only place, or even the most important place, in which Canadian anti-Americanism has manifested itself.

Rather, these moments of resistance to continental integration have been only part—and a relatively minor part—of much more consequential shifts in Canadian politics. It is hardly a coincidence that they went hand in hand with some of the truly constructive periods in our political history, with national unification in the nineteenth century and with Canada's development as a multinational, multicultural democracy in the twentieth. They grew from the same basic political motive, *refusal*: the recurring Canadian drive to gain a degree of economic and political separation from the hegemon, and the self-assurance it takes to realize that separation in practice. Economic determinism would tell us that that drive, in the long run, has mostly come to nothing. A more nuanced view would tell us that drives thwarted in one area of political life often make themselves felt in another.

We might revisit the Third Option with that view in mind—not because it was an economic success in its own terms, but because it recognized that economic terms are not the only ones that matter, that trade is not just trade. Sharp's critics were right to point out that his paper was a political document, not a real plan for policy. And while its lack of detail was certainly one cause of its failure as policy (perhaps even intentionally so), its treatment of trade as an extension of politics and culture was more than hot air. Trade policy truly can be a means to the end of "a more confident sense of national identity." In 1972, asserting Canadian identity looked like a way of resisting Nixonian "law and order" and the Southern Strategy, Agent Orange, and My Lai. Fifty years later, asserting Canadian identity looks like a way of resisting democratic erosion—or at least, that is the conviction behind this book. Our trade policy can still be, at least in part, a means to that end.

Even if trade policy is not the only, or the most effective, means to that end, conditions are in some ways riper for a Third Option today than they were fifty years ago. Despite the deep integration of the North American economy, protectionism is a rising force in American politics; in fact, it has been one of the most important continuities between the Trump and Biden administrations. In Canada as in many other countries, the pandemic, with its agonizing wait for vaccine shipments, was a powerful demonstration of the virtues of economic self-sufficiency, and the costs of its absence. Above all, the rise of markets that were still counted as "emerging" in 1972, along with the decline of the US economy in relative terms, makes the diversification of Canadian trade look far more plausible. In fact, the American share of Canadian trade has been steadily if gradually trending downwards since the 1990s, less through any deliberate policy than through the sort of amoral forces that thwarted the original Third Option.

If we were to update the Third Option for the twenty-first century, we ought to start with a serious degree of humility, a realistic sense of any Canadian government's ability, or willingness, to shape trade patterns to deliberate political ends. But with that caveat duly issued, I would propose three very broad principles for a renewed Third Option, a trade policy designed specifically around the problem of democratic erosion:

1. Trade is not just trade. Among many other things, it is a conduit for political ideas and practices. In an era of democratic decline, we can expect that it will increasingly be a conduit for authoritarian ideas and practices.

2. If trade is a conduit for ideas and practices, then trade with eroding democracies and nondemocracies is harmful to democracy. If America's democratic erosion continues, it is hard to imagine Canada's democracy remaining

unscathed as long as it remains in a position of economic dependency on America. Similarly, the events of the last generation have put the lie to the idea that integrating China into the world economy would promote democracy in China. In fact, it has had the opposite effect, weakening liberal and democratic values in China's trading partners (as when Hollywood movies are preemptively tailored to the taste of Chinese state censors). There is certainly no moral or political equivalence between an eroding America and an authoritarian China—but from the perspective of Canadian democracy, proximity matters, too. Sharing a border and a continental economy with an eroding democracy may in fact be more dangerous than trading across an ocean with a one-party state.

3. Given that we cannot forgo trading with eroding democracies and nondemocracies, diversification is crucial. Though we are in a period of worldwide democratic recession, failing democracies erode at different rates and through different, contingent events. Every unhappy democracy (Canada's included) is unhappy in its own way. We could think of diversifying our trade relationships, then, as a way of hedging against overexposure to any particular set of risks.

Third Option politics, whether in 1972 or the present, ask a great deal of us—in particular, to balance short-term economic interests against longer-term political interests. That has never been an easy request. And yet it may be somewhat easier now than it was fifty years ago. If diversifying away from the United States is more feasible today, it is also more important, because the political interests at stake are even greater—because entanglement with America exposes us to a distinctive set of risks.

Moreover, the Third Option is worth rearticulating as a guiding principle for Canada's relations with the world *even if* its economic impact proves as marginal as it did in the 1970s. The Third Option was essentially a political statement, and its restatement would be every bit as political today. It would be, now as then, a way of signalling that American influence on Canada cannot be shrugged off as basically benign.

If America stays on its current path of democratic instability and political violence, then I suspect we are only at the beginning of another period of Canadian anti-Americanism. In the years ahead, refusal may again become our dominant political theme. My hope is that we can also expect one of our great moments of political creativity and dynamism—a moment in which *not here* becomes an insistent motive for putting our own house in order.

I do not expect an era of unity and collaboration. That would be trivial. If we wanted that, it would be enough for our *not here* to be smug and self-satisfied in the worst Canadian tradition. I hope that our *not here* will be appropriately terrified. I hope for an era of bitterness, discord, and purpose—an era with the purposeful acrimony of the refounding. I hope that the stakes of our *not here* appear so high that no other political emotions will seem suitable.

One day, when the moment of creative refusal comes to an end and we take stock of the results, I hope that there is a permanent and formalized Indigenous role in the government of Canada; that the politics of *laïcité* will have been weighed against the prospects of a more robust social democracy, found wanting, and abandoned; that the role of prime minister is a newly humbled one, subject to meaningful controls by party caucuses, the cabinet, and Parliament as a whole; that we have an electoral system less archaic and less prone to alienate Canadians from their government than first past the post; and that we'll be reviewing the results of a series of more radical democratic experiments, such as the use of randomly selected citizens' assemblies to deliberate on laws, budgets, regulations, or constitutional reforms.

I hope for all those things, and more—but I also expect that no one person's opinion is going to count for much, not even the opinions of the most powerful. What strikes me about the refounding period is that it produced few, if any, outright political winners. None of its major players achieved all their aims. It came about through the mutual frustration of hopes—the hope for Indigenous assimilation, the hope for an independent Quebec, the hope for a new constitution satisfactory to all the provinces, the hope for economic independence from the United States—and yet it changed the face of the country nevertheless, in ways that none of the participants could have anticipated or planned. In just this way, none of my specific hopes for this country are worth much, except, perhaps, a very broad one: a period of intense care for and interest in Canadian democracy, which will make itself felt in any number of unpredictably creative acts.

There is a book about the far future by the great science fiction author Ursula K. Le Guin. It is a "fictional anthropology" of a people called the Kesh, who live some fifty thousand years from now in what was once the Napa Valley. By our technological standards, it is a chastened and reduced world, though not necessarily an unhappier one. Lacking much of our modern medicine, for instance, Kesh doctors rely on a practice called the "bringing-in," an exceptional period set aside for care and healing in the life of the sick person:

> The beneficial effect of a bringing-in lay to a great extent in *attention*—the attention paid to the *goddwe* [the brought-in, the sick person], who was the center of everybody's interest . . . and the attention which the *goddwe* must pay to his or her life and thinking and the mystical or intellectual or practical insights arrived at by the combined work of the people involved in the bringing-in. It was a pretty good example of what the Kesh meant by *uvrón*, carefulness, taking care.

It strikes me that, when it comes to democracy, we are more like the Kesh than we would like to admit. What we lack in science—in clear, objective answers for healing a sick country—we can make up for only in attention. "*Uvrón*, carefulness, taking care": something like that is what I want for this country.

———

Whatever kind of Canada emerges from that period of taking care, I expect its outward relationship with American power will remain much the same. Canadian prime ministers will still indiscriminately shake hands with American presidents, and if they sanitize afterwards, it will be off camera. There will still be the same banalities about friendship. And yet I hope they will increasingly be purposeful banalities, weapons of the weak that will protect our "not here."

If there are moments of confrontation, as inevitably crop up in any alliance, let them be *targeted* confrontations, chosen to vividly illustrate the difference between a multinational, multicultural democracy and the rule of the Real People. Consider a recent missed opportunity. Since 2004, Canada and the United States have been bound by the Safe Third Country Agreement, which mandates that refugees seek asylum in whichever of the two countries they first set foot in, on the assumption that both are equally "safe." In 2017, immigration activists renewed their calls for Canada to abandon the agreement, and to offer asylum to refugees who had transited through the United States to the Canadian border, because the United States had ceased to qualify as a safe haven. But even in the Trump years, the Trudeau government defended the agreement in Parliament and the courts. In the Biden years, it worked with the United States to make the agreement more restrictive. If you can imagine a future Canadian government doing just the opposite, you have a sense of what targeted confrontation might look like in practice.

What all of this amounts to is a policy of deliberate distancing from the United States (deliberate in both senses: *intentional* and *careful*). And yet I understand that I am giving this advice at a moment when it may sound especially perverse. As I write this, the most important story in Canada's foreign relations is its cooperation in the unprecedented NATO sanctions on Russia and in the American-led effort to channel weapons and aid to Ukraine. At the moment, Canada's collaboration with the United States is as tight as it has ever been in the post–World War II era—and, given the stakes of the Russian invasion of Ukraine for the state of democracy in the world, rightly so. Whatever the problems in American democracy, and however much those problems are magnified by proximity, they obviously pale in comparison with Vladimir Putin's regime. So Canada finds itself in a dilemma familiar to the middle powers of every era: as bad as "our" hegemon may be, the alternative is far worse. Isn't every confrontation with our allies a matter of aid and comfort to our enemies?

That is a pessimistic, zero-sum view of the world—but being pessimistic does not make it wrong. If it *is* wrong, I think its wrongness comes from not being pessimistic *enough*. What if, from the perspective of democracy, the game is better described as negative-sum—that is, a game that everyone is losing, only at different rates?

Two long-run facts speak for that view. First, it looks as if we are in the midst of a transition from a unipolar world dominated by the United States to a world polarized between the United States and its allies, on the one hand, and Russia and China, on the other. Second, this polarization is taking place against a backdrop of long-term democratic decline across the world—those sixteen consecutive years of democratic erosion as measured by Freedom House. Combined, these facts have some dire implications for a middle power like Canada. Even when it appropriately sides against the world's worst autocracies, there is no guarantee that its own democracy will be any better off as a result. The very presence of those autocracies on "the other side" renders Canada's own democracy worse off, because it creates a powerful incentive to ignore democratic erosion closer to home.

That is the destructive logic of great-power conflict, logic that has throttled democratic movements for centuries. In the nineteenth-century conflict between Britain and France, according to a recent historian, "legislation restricting freedom of speech, writing and assembly was passed in most parliamentary sessions from 1792 to 1801." In the birthplace of parliamentary liberalism, the authorities empowered themselves to arrest suspected radicals for any reason and to imprison them indefinitely without charges. That atmosphere of suspicion even found its way into Jane Austen novels. "Every man is surrounded by a neighbourhood of voluntary spies," a character tells the heroine of *Northanger Abbey*.

A little more than a century later, Germany's Social Democratic Party was the best-organized socialist party in the world. Improbably, this working-class party had come to control the largest bloc of seats in the Reichstag. Never had workers been so close to political power in western Europe. Yet in August 1914, the party gave in to the logic of great-power conflict and voted to support German entry into the Great War. It pledged not to call a strike or even so much as criticize the German government as long as the war lasted. "We will not desert our Fatherland in its hour of need," its chairman announced. The Social Democrats lived on as a centre-left party, and today they even lead Germany's governing coalition; but as a serious force for changing the world, they never recovered. The destructive phenomenon that Americans call "McCarthyism" is just one more instance of a sweeping problem: the potential of great-power conflict abroad to strangle democracy at home.

When Canada and its allies aid the defense of democracy in Ukraine, they are right to do so. But unless that defense comes complete with a plan to protect democracy at home from the dynamics of great-power conflict abroad, I'm worried that it will be self-defeating. I don't see any such plan in evidence, or even the sense that one might be needed, which strikes me as historical hubris on par with thinking in 2019 that global pandemics are a thing of the past.

In some regards, the domestic risks of great-power conflict may actually be more severe now than in the era of the Cold War. One silver lining of that period, as the legal scholar Derrick Bell famously and controversially argued, was America's temporary success in desegregating public schools. Desegregation was a powerful propaganda weapon against the Soviet adversary, whose own propaganda apparatus frequently played on the theme of American racial hypocrisy. And even though those Soviet claims were fundamentally self-serving, at least a little good came out of the fact that each great power had an interest in portraying itself as the superior advocate of human rights. In at least this one way, almost by accident, the terms of the conflict left some ordinary people better off (including my own mother, who was a white student in the first integrated high school class in Selma, Alabama).

Even when they are dishonest, the propaganda terms with which the great powers confront the world can have very real consequences. So it is decidedly another point for pessimism that Russia's propaganda terms are no longer faux egalitarian but faux Christian (and that China, too, paints its system of social control as a reaction to out-of-control Western liberalism). A year or two ago, it would have been an absurd fever dream to imagine a nuclear power piling civilians in mass graves in the name of the traditional gender binary. And yet, here is Putin in Red Square, defending his war: "Do we really want, here, in our country, in Russia, instead of 'mum' and 'dad,' to have 'parent number one,' 'parent number two,' 'number three'? Have they gone completely insane?" (Well, *someone* has.)

It is a message to Western publics as much as to Russians. And Western governments may well find themselves forced to grapple with—and to offer concessions to—the sizeable segments of their populations who find that message darkly appealing. If great-power conflict becomes, in its ideological aspect, a conflict over "traditional" social values, then national conservative movements across the Western countries will be well positioned to set the domestic agenda.

I've spoken of the "logic" of great-power conflict as if it's an impersonal force, not the result of the innumerable decisions of particular people. I've tried to do so deliberately, because I want to reflect the world as it looks from the perspective of a middle power like Canada. Our life in international politics is one long story of constraint, a continuous attempt to act with a degree of freedom and a degree of responsibility within structures so visibly built by others.

As much as we would like to believe that the future of Canadian democracy is entirely under Canadian control—and as much as I've erred on the side of that assumption in this book—there are important ways in which it simply is not. Democracy in Canada is weaker because democracy elsewhere, not least in America, is weaker. Whatever happens inside Canada, we will continue to be subject to oligarchic and authoritarian pressures from beyond our borders, as long as those pressures represent a powerful and growing force in the world. To the extent that we have an interest in democracy here, we have an interest in democracy elsewhere.

We live beside what is perhaps the world's most important case of democratic erosion, and because that is the case, Canadian localism—a sense of what sets us and our history and our political culture apart—is a necessary defense for our democracy. But that defense still requires partners. Canada is justly proud of its role in mediating the Suez Crisis in 1956 and in leading the negotiations for an international land mine ban in 1997: collaborative, multilateral efforts in which its role as a middle power was a help rather than a hindrance. A middle power is not simply an "honest broker," as the cliché goes—precisely because it lacks a hegemon's responsibilities, it can specialize in ways that a hegemon cannot.

Is there a more relevant place for Canada to specialize than in coordinating international work to secure the material basis of democracy? Closing tax shelters, taxing and expropriating oligarchic wealth, choking off the movement of laundered money through real estate and land markets (beginning in our own cities)—we could lead such a project with the authenticity of genuine self-interest. That project would not enable Canada to opt out of an era of great-power conflict. But it might, at its best, afford us moments of transcending that conflict, in the way that the countries of the Non-Aligned Movement sought to transcend the Cold War. Those moments would demonstrate that democracy can be served and advanced outside the bounds of the conflict, that the success of democracy is not synonymous with the victory of either side.

Yet to be a middle power is to accept that there is no such thing as complete autonomy for us. There never will be. Certainly not in our relations with the world, and not even in our domestic politics, which have been shaped by the presence of our hegemon since before Confederation, and which will continue to be distorted by great-power conflicts that we did little or nothing to bring about.

In some sense, constraints like those weigh on all of us, even the great powers themselves: we are all bound by facts not of our making. Maybe one thing that separates the middle or lesser from the great powers is the degree to which they have taken that idea to heart and allowed it to permeate their politics. If the beginning of wisdom in individual life is coming to terms with the fact of your death, maybe the beginning of wisdom in political life is coming to terms with the limits of your power. Maybe this is one advantage, however dubious, of living in the American shadow.

Conclusion

HERE

I'VE NEVER BEEN ABLE TO draw much beyond a stick fig-ure. But if I could, I'm sure I could re-create from memory a particular campsite on the southern end of Algonquin Provincial Park. My family began canoe camping there at the start of the pandemic, and, being creatures of habit, we've been back each summer since.

It does not strike me as an extraordinary place. Its best features are a little sandy shore and, up a small in-cline, a wooded section full of evenly spaced birch trees and absolutely nothing else, as if a giant gardener had pulled the rest out by the roots. The sand makes a good place for the grown-ups to beach the canoe and for the kids to splash and collect rocks, and the stand of trees is shaded, cool, and uncanny, but I know that that same modest and unspectacular scene is repeated with minor variations thousands of times from one end of Algon-quin to another. And when I add up the days we've spent there, they come to less than a week. Yet I have a better spatial sense for this place than for some neighbourhoods where I lived for years.

It has been incised into my memory at a surprising depth, not because it is inherently very memorable, not because anything especially remarkable happened there, but only because I paid attention. What else is there to do on a camping trip? You pitch a tent, you make a fire, you cook and eat, and you pay very close attention to a very small space—the kind of intensity of attention it is so much harder to pay in places where the world presses in more closely. On our second or third night there, I made the mistake of leaving my flashlight in the tent, and after I put out the fire I realized that the light on my phone had died. It was overcast and solid black, and the tent was somewhere farther back from the shore in the dark. After some mild panic, we decided to all link arms so no one would be lost, and we set off in what seemed to be the most likely direction. We tripped on roots and bumped into trees until my daughter's outstretched leg kicked the rain fly, and we were home. With enough attention, it turned out, we could learn a place well enough to navigate it in the dark.

I've spent years trying to learn this larger place, Canada, but I will never know it in that same assured, painstaking way. I will never know it, as it were, with the balls of my feet—not because I am a newcomer, but because these are categorically different ways of knowing, and it is impossible to know a country in the same way you can know any given piece of it. As with quantum mechanics, the rules change as the scale changes.

It was once a profound insight, and is now mostly received wisdom, that modern countries are "imagined communities." They are different from the communities we have no need to imagine, the neighbours we know face-to-face, the spaces and land we can know with the kind of bodily immediacy that I felt for a moment at that campsite in the dark. The country itself is in none of those places: it is an image layered atop them, like a transparency slide or the view through an augmented-reality screen. And it is nonetheless as real, as consequential, as our most potent shared stories. The stand of birch trees and the country of which they are a part: two different orders of reality.

No doubt there was once a time when it was disorienting, nauseating, for the average person to move back and forth between those realities. Now most of us make that transition dozens of times each day without a second thought, aided by the technologies of flag and anthem, of national teams and hard currency, of mass media and passports and citizenship oaths. For some, because countries are imagined, dreams foisted on us by our rulers for their own purposes, we should work to wake up from them. For others, because they are communities, the broadest experience of solidarity that most of us will ever know, we should kill and die for them. For still others, because they are simply dangerous and powerful facts of this world, we should above all approach them with care. That is what I have tried to do in this book. "*Uvrón*, carefulness, taking care": recognizing our complicated feelings for this place, turning them over in our hands, and then trying to put them to use.

All of that is harder in Canada, here on the empire's edge. *Where is here?* That, Northrop Frye claimed, is the essential Canadian question. It is not a question about the physical immediacy of this place, but about the other, imagined place. It is a question that confronts us with our disunity, with our paucity of stories, with our unthinking tendency to imagine ourselves into America while the ground right here is shifting beneath our feet. But it is also the sort of disoriented sleepwalker's question that melts and dissolves when the right amount of attention is applied. Here is here.

The stand of birch trees and the country of which they are a part: incommensurable, except for the way our attention transforms them, and perhaps us. In my years as a newcomer, Canada has absorbed me and disappointed me and consoled me—has consoled me above all, has kept me sane and whole, an unasked-for gift, through a dark time in the country of my birth.

And where is *there?* Our neighbour is struggling mightily to refound itself. May it be done in my lifetime. May it be done before my children are old.

Acknowledgments

I WAS FORTUNATE ENOUGH TO write most of this book out-
doors during the warmer months, in public parks. If it were
possible to thank a place, I would start with Greenwood Park
and Withrow Park in Toronto, and Carré Saint-Louis and
Parc La Fontaine in Montreal. But it would be better to thank
the city planners who designed them, the workers who built
and continue to maintain them, the community groups that
advocate for their funding and those politicians who listen to
them, and the many people who shared these public spaces
with me. I would like to think that some of those spaces' best
qualities—their grace, their openness, and their liberality—
made their way by osmosis into what I wrote there. But even
if not, a writer always needs a model to strive for.

I also want to thank the friends whose conversations and
comments helped to improve this book: they include John
Beebe, Sasha Dyck, Dora-Marie Goulet, Evan Light, Joanne
Penhale, and Jennifer London. Thanks as well to our community of G.G. and Plum Place friends, who make me and

my family feel at home here—a necessary condition for writing this. My academic community of scholars and students at Toronto Metropolitan University has been just as important in that regard. Ben Wolinsky, who grew up in Winnipeg, was responsible for my superlative first impression of Canada, long before I moved here. I want to thank him for more than two decades of friendship, and for being the first person to encourage me to write about my new country.

Justin Stoller, my editor at Simon & Schuster Canada, improved this book to a remarkable extent with his attentive reading and his thoughtful comments—and beyond that, his belief in this project, from first pitch to final draft, was absolutely infectious. Thanks as well to Janie Yoon and Karen Silva at Simon & Schuster Canada for supporting this project from the outset and for helping me to carry it through to completion, and to Douglas Johnson for his diligent copyediting. Thanks to Ben Woodfinden for his fact-checking assistance. And thanks to my agent, Laura Yorke: after more than a decade of working with her, it's still magical to me to be able to call her up with an idea and see it turn into a book some time later.

While nearly all immigration stories involve more difficulty or danger than mine, leaving one's home and making a new one is never a little thing. So my last and most important thanks are to my wife, Ellen, and our daughters, for all they have done, and for all they do every day, to build a home here with me.

Toronto/Montreal
2022–23

Notes

EPIGRAPH

ix *"There is a certain bleakness"*: Ursula K. Le Guin, *The Farthest Shore* (New York: Atheneum, 2012 [1972]), 45.

INTRODUCTION

6 *"the impossibility of Canada"*: George Grant, *Lament for a Nation: The Defeat of Canadian Nationalism* (Montreal: McGill-Queens University Press, 2005 [1965]), 67.

6 *"senior founding pillar"*: John Ralston Saul, *A Fair Country: Telling Truths about Canada* (Toronto: Penguin Canada, 2008), 21.

7 *"Canada moved from colony"*: Harold A. Innis, "Great Britain, the United States and Canada," in Harold A. Innis, *Essays in Canadian Economic History*, ed. Mary Q. Innis, (Toronto: University of Toronto Press, 1956), 404–5.

7 *"We have been (and are)"*: Margaret Atwood, *Survival: A Thematic Guide to Canadian Literature* (Toronto: House of Anansi Press, 2012 [1972]), 38.

7   *"is practically the only country"*: Northrop Frye, "Author's Preface," in Northrop Frye, *The Bush Garden: Essays on the Canadian Imagination* (Toronto: House of Anansi Press, 2017 [1971]), 36.

7   *"no history of colonialism"*: David Ljunggren, "Every G20 Nation Wants to Be Canada, PM Insists," Reuters, September 25, 2009, https://www.reuters.com/article/columns-us-g20-canada-advantages-idUSTRE58P05Z20090926.

8   *"We are to the Americans"*: Atwood, *Survival*, 106.

8   *It has rendered our nationalism*: See Andrew Potter, "Who Loves Canada?," *The Line* (newsletter), February 28, 2021, https://theline.substack.com/p/andrew-potter-who-loves-canada.

8   *"How is it"*: Samuel Johnson, *Taxation No Tyranny* (London: T. Cadell, 1775), 89.

10 *"What is resented"*: Frye, "Author's Preface," 37.

11 *two hundred election-denying Republicans*: Karen Yourish et al., "See Which 2020 Election Deniers and Skeptics Won and Lost in the Midterm Elections," *New York Times*, November 10, 2022, https://www.nytimes.com/interactive/2022/11/09/us/politics/election-misinformation-midterms-results.html.

11 *nineteen states responded*: "Voting Laws Roundup: December 2021," Brennan Center for Justice, December 21, 2021, https://www.brennancenter.org/our-work/research-reports/voting-laws-roundup-december-2021.

11 *House elections*: Bloomberg News deemed the 2022 House elections "surprisingly competitive" because roughly 8 percent of races were decided by a margin of five percentage points or less. Over the past two decades, an average of just 6 percent of all House races have been similarly competitive. Gregory Korte, Leonardo Nicoletti, and Andre Tartar, "Why the Fight for the House Was Surprisingly Competitive," Bloomberg, Novem-

ber 18, 2022, https://www.bloomberg.com/graphics/2022-mid
term-election-polarization-fate-of-competitive-seats.

12 *"It's time for us"*: Catherine Porter, "Trudeau's 21-Second Pause
Becomes the Story in Canada," *New York Times*, June 3, 2020,
https://www.nytimes.com/2020/06/03/world/canada/trudeau
-canada-george-floyd-protests.html.

12 *"First Amendment?"*: Stephanie Taylor, Mike Blanchfield, and
Erika Ibrahim, "Ottawa Police Push Ahead to End Protest as Bail
Hearings for Organizers Move Forward," *Toronto Star*, February 19, 2022, https://www.thestar.com/politics/2022/02/19
/massive-police-action-continuing-in-ottawa-to-end-occupa
tion.html.

13 *"We are glad"*: Brian Gabrial, " 'The Second American Revolution': Expressions of Canadian Identity in News Coverage at
the Outbreak of the United States Civil War," *Canadian Journal
of Communication* 33 (2008): 21–37.

14 *The RCMP swayed*: Richard Brennan, "RCMP Likely Swayed
Federal Election, Report Says," *Toronto Star*, April 1, 2008,
https://www.thestar.com/news/canada/2008/04/01/rcmp_likely
_swayed_federal_election_report_says.html.

15 *sixteen consecutive years*: Sarah Repucci and Amy Slipowitz,
*Freedom in the World 2022: The Global Expansion of Authori-
tarian Rule* (Washington, DC: Freedom House, February 2022),
https://freedomhouse.org/sites/default/files/2022-02/FIW
_2022_PDF_Booklet_Digital_Final_Web.pdf. At the same
time, claims of global democratic erosion have also been contested by some political scientists. For a summary, see Hélène
Landemore, *Open Democracy: Reinventing Popular Rule for
the Twenty-First Century* (Princeton, NJ: Princeton University
Press, 2020), 26–31.

15 *alleged Chinese interference*: John Paul Tasker, "MPs Agree to Probe Allegations of Chinese Interference in Federal Elections," CBC News, November 14, 2022, https://www.cbc.ca/news/politics/mps-probe-chinese-interference-elections-1.6651121.

15 *44 percent of funding*: Richard Lardner, Michelle R. Smith, and Ali Swenson, "U.S. Funds for Ottawa Trucker Convoy Protests May Sway American Politics Too," *Globe and Mail*, February 17, 2022, https://www.theglobeandmail.com/world/article-us-funds-for-canadian-convoy-protests-may-sway-american-politics-too.

16 *"The United States is and will remain"*: Vincent Rigby et al., *A National Security Strategy for the 2020s: How Canada Can Adapt to a Deteriorating Security Environment* (University of Ottawa, Graduate School of Public and International Affairs, Task Force on National Security, May 2022), https://socialsciences.uottawa.ca/public-international-affairs/sites/socialsciences.uottawa.ca.public-international-affairs/files/natsec_report_gspia_may2022.pdf, 6.

16 *"There are serious risks"*: Thomas Juneau, quoted in Catharine Tunney, "Canada Should Rethink Relationship with U.S. as Democratic 'Backsliding' Worsens: Security Experts," CBC News, May 24, 2022, https://www.cbc.ca/news/politics/national-security-us-fox-news-threat-report-1.6459660.

20 *"are capable of describing"*: B. Van Stolk and C. Wouters, "Power Changes and Self-Respect: A Comparison of Two Cases of Established-Outsiders Relations," *Theory, Culture and Society* 4, nos. 2–3 (1987): 477–88.

21 *"The union is only possible"* . . . *"Without it"*: Timothy Messer-Kruse, "The Unbearable Whiteness of Ken Burns," *Chronicle of Higher Education*, April 20, 2022, https://www.chronicle.com/article/the-unbearable-whiteness-of-ken-burns.

Notes

22 structures of refusal: David Graeber and David Wengrow, *The Dawn of Everything: A New History of Humanity* (New York: Farrar, Straus and Giroux, 2021), 174.

CHAPTER 1: FOUNDINGS

29 *"You're the real people"*: Brian Naylor, "Read Trump's Jan. 6 Speech, a Key Part of Impeachment Trial," NPR, February 10, 2021, https://www.npr.org/2021/02/10/966396848/read-trumps -jan-6-speech-a-key-part-of-impeachment-trial.

31 *an irreducible gap*: For the contrast of the people as a "political principle," and the people as a "sociological principle," see Pierre Rosanvallon, *Democracy Past and Future* (New York: Columbia University Press, 2006), 37, 469. See also Rosanvallon, *La démocratie inachevée: Histoire de la souveraineté du peuple en France* (Paris: Gallimard, 2000); Oliver Flügel-Martinsen et al., ed., *Pierre Rosanvallon's Political Thought: Interdisciplinary Approaches* (Bielefeld: Bielefeld University Press, 2019), 49; Edmund S. Morgan, *Inventing the People* (New York: W. W. Norton, 1987); Melvin Rogers, "The People, Rhetoric, and Affect: On the Political Force of Du Bois's *The Souls of Black Folk*," *American Political Science Review* 106, no. 1 (2012): 188–203.

31 *"What is the Third Estate?"*: Abbe Sieyès, "What Is the Third Estate?" in *Political Writings* (Indianapolis: Hackett, 2003 [1789]), 92.

33 *"Was it proper"*: W. E. B. Du Bois, *Black Reconstruction in America* (New Brunswick, NJ: Transaction, 2013 [1935]), 265–66. The line beginning "Was it proper . . ." is Du Bois's paraphrase of Johnson. The rest of the exchange is quoted verbatim.

34 *"He is not pretending"*: George Orwell, *1984* (New York: Harcourt, 2003 [1949]), 331.

35 *"The larger implication"*: Jamelle Bouie, "Politics," in *The 1619 Project: A New Origin Story*, ed. Nikole Hannah-Jones et al. (New York: One World, 2021), 207.

37 *In Georgia, Republican lawmakers*: David Wickert and Mark Niesse, "Ban on Distributing Food and Water at Georgia Polls Upheld," *Atlanta Journal-Constitution*, August 19, 2022, https://www.ajc.com/politics/food-and-water-ban-at-the-polls-upheld-in-georgia-elections/XQVWU5KSXFC4JN7JLKSBKV2LSI.

37 *In Florida, an overwhelming majority*: German Lopez, "Florida Votes to Restore Ex-Felon Voting Rights with Amendment 4," *Vox*, November 7, 2018, https://www.vox.com/policy-and-politics/2018/11/6/18052374/florida-amendment-4-felon-voting-rights-results.

37 *imposing poll taxes*: Robert P. Alvarez, "Return of the Poll Tax," *Otherwords*, July 10, 2019, https://otherwords.org/return-of-the-poll-tax.

37 *highly publicized arrests*: Tim Craig and Lori Rozsa, "Florida Let Them Vote. Then DeSantis's Election Police Arrested Them," *Washington Post*, September 4, 2022, https://www.washingtonpost.com/nation/2022/09/04/desantis-election-police-voter-arrests/.

38 *Political scientists have concluded*: David Daley and Gaby Goldstein, "America Is Full of Democracy Deserts," *The Guardian*, August 13, 2021, https://www.theguardian.com/commentisfree/2021/aug/13/america-is-full-of-democracy-deserts-wisconsin-rivals-congo-on-some-metrics. See Pippa Norris, Electoral Integrity in the 2020 U.S. Elections, Electoral Integrity Project,

December 1, 2020, https://www.electoralintegrityproject.com /peius2020; Holly Ann Garnett, Toby S. James, and Madison MacGregor, Electoral Integrity Global Report 2019-2021, Electoral Integrity Project, May 2022, https://www.electoralintegrity project.com/globalreport2019-2021.

38 *By gutting the Voting Rights Act*: Ari Berman, "Eight Years Ago, the Supreme Court Gutted the Voting Rights Act. Widespread Voter Suppression Resulted," *Mother Jones*, June 25, 2021, https://www .motherjones.com/politics/2021/06/eight-years-ago-the-supreme -court-gutted-the-voting-rights-act-widespread-voter-suppres sion-resulted; Elie Mystal, "'It Could Have Been Worse' Is the Wrong Response to the Midterms," *The Nation*, November 10, 2022, https://www.thenation.com/article/politics/gerrymandering-re publican-victories-midterms. For a more optimistic discussion, emphasizing the growth of nonpartisan redistricting commissions (along with the Supreme Court's continued threat to free and fair elections), see Robert J. Shapiro, "The Decline and Possible Resurrection of Radical Gerrymandering," *Washington Monthly*, January 4, 2023, https://washingtonmonthly.com/2023/01/04 /the-decline-and-possible-resurrection-of-radical-gerrymandering.

38 *Republicans have openly defied*: Michael Wines, "Maps in Four States Were Ruled Illegal Gerrymanders. They're Being Used Anyway," *New York Times*, April 8, 2022, https://www.nytimes .com/2022/08/08/us/elections/gerrymandering-maps-elections -republicans.html.

39 *"far and away"*: David Leonhardt, "'A Crisis Coming': The Twin Threats to American Democracy," *New York Times*, September 17, 2022, https://www.nytimes.com/2022/09/17/us /american-democracy-threats.html.

39 *The 2020 election*: Ian Millhiser, "America's Anti-Democratic

Senate, in One Number," *Vox*, January 6, 2021, https://www
.vox.com/2021/1/6/22215728/senate-anti-democratic-one
-number-raphael-warnock-jon-ossoff-georgia-runoffs.

39 *The Senate filibuster*: As of the 2020 Census, the forty senators
from the twenty least populous states represented just under
thirty-four million Americans, about 10 percent of the total
population. While it is unlikely that all forty small-state senators
would vote together, that hypothetical does illustrate the depth
of the Senate's antimajoritarian bias.

39 *explicitly impossible to amend*: Specifically, "no State, without
its Consent, shall be deprived of its equal Suffrage in the Senate"
[article V].

39 *By 2040, it is projected*: Philip Bump, "By 2040, Two-Thirds
of America Will Be Represented by 30 Percent of the Senate,"
Washington Post, November 28, 2017, https://www.washington
post.com/news/politics/wp/2017/11/28/by-2040-two-thirds
-of-americans-will-be-represented-by-30-percent-of-the-senate.

40 *regular threats of prison rape*: Ryan Bort and Asawin Suebsa-
eng, "Trump Keeps Musing about Journalists Being Raped in
Prison—He's Not Joking," *Rolling Stone*, November 8, 2022,
https://www.rollingstone.com/politics/politics-news/trump
-imagines-journalists-raped-prison-1234626493.

40 *"Second Amendment people"*: Nick Corasaniti and Maggie
Haberman, "Trump Suggests 'Second Amendment People'
Could Act against Clinton," *New York Times*, August 6, 2016,
https://www.nytimes.com/2016/08/10/us/politics/donald
-trump-hillary-clinton.html.

40 *"trial by combat"*: Katelyn Polantz, "Giuliani, Who Urged
Trump Supporters to Have 'Trial by Combat,' Says He Wasn't
Literally Calling for Insurrection," CNN, May 18, 2021, https://

www.cnn.com/2021/05/18/politics/rudy-giuliani-january-6 -insurrection-lawsuit/index.html.

40 *Some of this violence*: See, for example, Rebekah Reiss and Dakin Andone, "School Mask Debate in Tennessee Grows Heated as Local Board Requires Masks in Elementary Schools," CNN, August 12, 2021, https://www.cnn.com/2021/08/12/ten nessee-covid-mask-mandate-school-board-protest/index.html; Hannah Natanson, "Death Threats, Online Abuse, Police Protection: School Board Members Face Dark New Reality," *Washington Post*, November 9, 2021, https://www.washingtonpost.com /local/education/death-threats-online-abuse-police-protection -school-board-members-face-dark-new-reality/2021/11/09 /db007706-37fe-11ec-9bc4-86107e7b0ab1_story.html; Gabriella Borter, Joseph Ax, and Joseph Tanfani, "School Boards Get Death Threats Amid Rage over Race, Gender, Mask Policies," Reuters, February 15, 2022, https://www.reuters.com/investigates/special -report/usa-education-threats; Catie Edmonson, " 'There Is No-where I Feel Safe': Election Officials Describe Threats Fueled by Trump," *New York Times*, June 21, 2022, https://www.nytimes .com/2022/06/21/us/politics/jan-6-trump-threats.html.

40 *"You will all be executed"* . . . *"Wire around their limbs"*: Lindo So, Peter Eisler, and Jason Szep, " 'Kill Them': Arizona Election Workers Face Midterm Threats," Reuters, November 6, 2022, https://www.reuters.com/world/us/kill-them-arizona-election -workers-face-midterm-threats-2022-11-06.

40 *"I KNOW WHERE YOU SLEEP"*: Cat Zakrzewski, "Election Workers Brace for Torrent of Threats: 'I KNOW WHERE YOU SLEEP,' " *Washington Post*, November 8, 2022, https:// www.washingtonpost.com/technology/2022/11/08/election -workers-online-threats.

40 *"It is not the creature"*: Ida B. Wells, "Lynch Law in America," *The Arena* 23 (January 1900): 15.

41 *"the fever may break"*: Byron Tau, "Obama: Republican 'Fever' Will Break after the Election," *Politico*, June 1, 2012, https://www .politico.com/blogs/politico44/2012/06/obama-republican -fever-will-break-after-the-election-125059.

41 *"Republicans will never lose"*: Martin Pengelly, "Republican Says Party 'Will Never Lose Another Election' in Wisconsin If He Wins," *The Guardian*, November 2, 2022, https://www .theguardian.com/us-news/2022/nov/02/wisconsin-republican -gubernatorial-candidate-tim-michels.

41 *"We only have to be lucky"*: Peter Taylor, *Brits: The War against the IRA* (London: Bloomsbury, 2017), 265.

41 *"battle for the soul"*: Alexander Burns, "Joe Biden's Campaign Announcement Video, Annotated," *New York Times*, April 25, 2019, https://www.nytimes.com/2019/04/25/us/politics/biden -campaign-video-announcement.html.

41 *"moments so stark"*: "Remarks by Joe Biden on Protect-ing the Right to Vote," January 11, 2022, Atlanta University Center Consortium, Atlanta, https://www.whitehouse.gov /briefing-room/speeches-remarks/2022/01/11/remarks-by -president-biden-on-protecting-the-right-to-vote.

41 *"semi-fascism"*: Christopher Cadelago and Olivia Olander, "Biden Calls Trump's Philosophy 'Semi-Fascism,'" *Politico*, August 25, 2022, https://www.politico.com/news/2022/08/25 /biden-trump-philosophy-semi-fascism-00053831.

43 *"That's been the history"*: Ezra Klein, "Obama Explains How We Went from 'Yes We Can' to 'MAGA,'" *New York Times*, June 1, 2021, https://www.nytimes.com/2021/06/01/opinion /ezra-klein-podcast-barack-obama.html.

Notes

43 *some two dozen occasions*: See the Obama White House digital archives: search.archives.gov/search?query=%22two+steps+forward%22&op=Search&affiliate=obamawhitehouse.

46 *so many violent threats*: Daniel Leblanc, "RCMP Running Short of Officers to Protect Cabinet Ministers from a Growing Number of Threats," CBC News, October 26, 2022, https://www.cbc.ca/news/politics/rcmp-close-protection-unit-shortage-cabinet-prime-minister-threats-1.6629092.

46 *"old-stock Canadians"*: Mark Gollom, "Stephen Harper's 'Old-Stock Canadians': Politics of Division or Simple Slip," CBC News, September 19, 2015, https://www.cbc.ca/news/politics/old-stock-canadians-stephen-harper-identity-politics-1.3234386.

48 *honoured predecessors*: There were some references to a *"deuxième république"* in 1848, but the term *"troisième république"* is much more common after 1870. Thanks to Dan Edelstein for this information.

48 *Russia has been refounded*: See Timothy Snyder, "We Should Say It. Russia Is Fascist," *New York Times*, May 19, 2022, https://www.nytimes.com/2022/05/19/opinion/russia-fascism-ukraine-putin.html.

48 *"destitute of all"*: Gerald M. Craig, ed., *Lord Durham's Report* (Kingston, ON: McGill-Queen's University Press, 2007), 31, 149. Cited in Peter H. Russell, *Canada's Odyssey: A Country Based on Incomplete Conquests* (Toronto: University of Toronto Press, 2017), 110.

49 *"do hereby cede"*: A standard clause in the numbered treaties between 1871 and 1921; see Russell, Canada's Odessey, 184.

49 *"abhorrent to the Aryan race"*: Aaron Wherry, "Was John A. Macdonald a White Supremacist?" *Maclean's*, August 21, 2021, https://www.macleans.ca/politics/ottawa/was-john-a-macdonald-a-white-supremacist.

50 *"incomplete conquests"*: Russell, *Canada's Odyssey*, 4.

Notes

51   *a third of Canadians*: See David Coletto (@DavidColetto), July 20, 2022, 10:47 a.m., Twitter, https://twitter.com/DavidColetto /status/1553391775036985345 (the poll was conducted by Abacus Data).

54   *triple its population*: John Ibbitson, "It's Time for Canada to Focus on Expanding Our Population," *Globe and Mail*, March 31, 2021, https://www.theglobeandmail.com/politics /article-its-time-for-canada-to-focus-on-expanding-our-popu lation.

54   *plans for half a million new immigrants*: Randy Thanthong-Knight, "Trudeau Plans Record Number of Immigrants to Canada Through 2024," Bloomberg, February 14, 2022, https:// www.bloomberg.com/news/articles/2022-02-14/trudeau -plans-record-number-of-immigrants-to-canada-through-2024.

54   *Pierre Poilievre launches*: Ben Woodfinden, "Canada's Aspiring Populists Aren't Actually All that Radical," *The Hub*, May 27, 2022, https://thehub.ca/2022-05-27/canadas-aspiring-populists -arent-actually-all-that-radical.

54   *footage of migrant "caravans"*: For the Fox News archive of "Migrant Caravan" coverage, see https://www.foxnews.com /category/world/migrant-caravan.

54   *Australia detains migrants*: "Australia Ends Controversial Asylum Detention Deal with Papua New Guinea," BBC, October 6, 2021, https://www.bbc.com/news/world-australia-58812578.

54   *billboard vans*: Simon Hattenstone, "Why Was the Scheme Behind May's 'Go Home' Vans Called Operation Vaken?" *The Guardian*, April 26, 2018, https://www.theguardian.com/com mentisfree/2018/apr/26/theresa-may-go-home-vans-operation -vaken-ukip.

55   *highest naturalization rate*: Jonathan Tepperman, "Eye for Tal-

ent: Why Canada Wins at Immigration," *The Walrus*, October 18, 2016, https://thewalrus.ca/eye-for-talent; Immigration, Refugees and Citizenship Canada, "#ImmigrationMatters: Canada's Immigration Track Record," September 7, 2022, https://www.canada.ca/en/immigration-refugees-citizenship/campaigns/immigration-matters/track-record.html.

55 *a political struggle against homogeneity*: See Charles Foran, "The Canada Experiment: Is This the World's First 'Postnational' Country?," *The Guardian*, January 4, 2017, https://www.theguardian.com/world/2017/jan/04/the-canada-experiment-is-this-the-worlds-first-postnational-country.

56 *"a non-racial idea"*: John Ralston Saul, *A Fair Country: Telling Truths about Canada* (Toronto: Penguin Canada, 2008), 4, 20.

56 *a truth already widely known*: See Bob Joseph, *21 Things You May Not Know about the Indian Act* (Saanichton, BC: Indigenous Relations Press, 2018), 53–54.

57 *"is to play the imperialists' game"*: Tony Judt, *Postwar: A History of Europe Since 1945* (New York: Penguin, 2005), 212.

57 *"The illusion that Communism was reformable"*: Ibid. 447.

58 *"to wean them"*: E. B. Biggar, *Anecdotal Life of Sir John Macdonald* (Montreal: John Lovell & Son, 1891), 177.

58 *"Canada has become"*: Leanne Betasamosake Simpson, *As We Have Always Done: Indigenous Freedom through Radical Resistance* (Minneapolis: University of Minnesota Press, 2017), 239.

59 *Second Reconstruction*: The term was coined by the historian C. Vann Woodward in *The Strange Career of Jim Crow* (New York: Oxford University Press, 2001 [1955]). See Kevin K. Gaines, "The End of the Second Reconstruction," *Modern American History* 1, no. 1 (2018): 113–19. On this period as a "refounding" for the United States, see Danielle S. Allen, *Talking*

to Strangers: Anxieties of Citizenship Since Brown v. Board of Education (Chicago: University of Chicago Press, 2004), 7.

60 *"When the architects"*: Martin Luther King Jr., "I Have a Dream," in *Testament of Hope: The Essential Writings and Speeches of Martin Luther King, Jr.*, ed. James Melvin Washington (New York: HarperCollins, 1986), 217.

61 *"a constant widening"*: "President Obama's Farewell Address," Chicago, January 10, 2017, https://obamawhitehouse.archives .gov/farewell.

61 *"nations within"*: Russell, *Canada's Odyssey*, 3.

61 *largely displaced a competing vision*: This is not to imply that the outcome was the result of some disinterested contest in the marketplace of ideas, given that Black movements and leaders of the Second Reconstruction, of all political stripes, were the targets of federal surveillance, interference, and violence.

61 *"a Negro nation"*: W. E. B. Du Bois, "A Negro Nation within a Nation," in *Ripples of Hope: Great American Civil Rights Speeches*, ed. Josh Gottheimer (New York: Basic Civitas Books, 2003), 172. I discuss Du Bois's turn to separatism in "The Rhetorical Roots of Du Bois's Double Consciousness," in *History of Political Thought* (forthcoming). See also Joseph P. DeMarco, "The Rationale and Foundation of Du Bois's Theory of Economic Cooperation," *Phylon* 35, no. 1 (1975): 5–15; Andrew Douglas, *W. E. B. Du Bois and the Critique of the Competitive Society* (Athens: University of Georgia Press, 2019); David Levering Lewis, *W.E.B. Du Bois: A Biography, 1868–1963* (New York: Henry Holt, 2009), 574.

62 *"foundations are laid"*: Alexander H. Stephens, "The 'Cornerstone' Speech," March 21, 1861, https://www.blackpast.org/african-amer ican-history/1861-alexander-h-stephens-cornerstone-speech/.

Notes

62 *"pillory [a] great section"*: Robert A. Caro, *The Years of Lyndon Johnson*, vol. 3, *Master of the Senate* (New York: Vintage, 2003), 184.

64 "One will see great desire": Niccolò Machiavelli, *Discourses on Livy*, trans. Harvey C. Mansfield and Nathan Tarcov (Chicago: University of Chicago Press, 1996), 18.

64 *The Southern Strategy*: On "the nationalization of the South's reactionary minoritarian techniques," see Rick Perlstein, "This Is Us: Why the Trump Era Ended in Violence," *New Republic*, January 20, 2021, https://newrepublic.com/article/160975/trump-era-always-going-end-violence.

66 *"American politics today"*: George Packer, "A New Report Offers Insights into Tribalism in the Age of Trump," *New Yorker*, October 13, 2018, https://www.newyorker.com/news/daily-comment/a-new-report-offers-insights-into-tribalism-in-the-age-of-trump.

67 *"Black power through Black majorities"*: Charles Blow, "We Need a Second Great Migration," *New York Times*, January 8, 2021, https://www.nytimes.com/2021/01/08/opinion/georgia-black-political-power.html. See also Charles Blow, *The Devil You Know: A Black Power Manifesto* (New York: Harper, 2021).

67 *"What I sometimes tell my staff"*: Alexandria Ocasio-Cortez (@AOC), June 24, 2022, 10:36 a.m., Twitter, https://twitter.com/AOC/status/1540343019966185472.

68 *"Your purpose, then"*: Abraham Lincoln, "Address at Cooper Institute, New York City," in *Collected Works of Abraham Lincoln*, ed. Roy P. Basler et al. (New Brunswick, NJ: Rutgers University Press, 1953), 3:543.

69 *"require dealing with the hard stuff"*: Russell, *Canada's Odyssey*, 438–39.

69 *assignment of reconciliation to the category of liberal do-goodism*: See Martin Lukacs, "Reconciliation: The False Promise of Trudeau's Sunny Ways," *The Walrus*, September 19, 2019, https://thewalrus.ca/the-false-promise-of-trudeaus-sunny-ways.

70 *"Aboriginal nationalists" . . . "possess unique forms of rights"*: Dale Turner, *This Is Not a Peace Pipe: Towards a Critical Indigenous Philosophy* (Toronto: University of Toronto Press, 2006), 5, 73.

70 *"I believe my Ancestors"*: Simpson, *As We Have Always Done*, 9.

71 *the severe damage*: See, for example, Tom Phillips, "'Bolsonaro's to Blame': Indigenous Rights Champion on Crisis in Brazil," *The Guardian*, August 30, 2022, https://www.theguardian.com/world/2022/aug/30/sydney-possuelo-brazil-indigenous-people-interview-bolsonaro; Marcia Reverdosa, Sahar Akbarzai, and Camilo Rocha, "Invasions and Illegal Exploitation of Indigenous Lands in Brazil Tripled under Bolsonaro, Says Advocacy Group," CNN, August 28, 2022, https://www.cnn.com/2022/08/28/americas/brazil-land-invasions-bolsonaro-latam-intl/index.html; Annette McGivney, "Outcry as Trump Officials to Transfer Sacred Native American Land to Miners," *The Guardian*, January 16, 2021, https://www.theguardian.com/environment/2021/jan/16/sacred-native-american-land-arizona-oak-flat; Anna V. Smith, "Trump's Impact on Indian Country over Four Years," *High Country News*, December 16, 2020, https://www.hcn.org/articles/indigenous-affairs-trumps-impact-on-indian-country-over-four-years; Julie Turkewitz, "Trump Slashes Size of Bears Ears and Grand Staircase Monuments," *New York Times*, December 4, 2017, https://www.nytimes.com/2017/12/04/us/trump-bears-ears.html.

71 *provincial equalization payments*: This was one of the recommendations of the 1996 Royal Commission on Aboriginal Peo-

ples. *Report of the Royal Commission on Aboriginal Peoples*, 2:273, https://www.bac-lac.gc.ca/eng/discover/aboriginal-heri tage/royal-commission-aboriginal-peoples/Pages/final-report .aspx. See also Douglas Sanderson, "A Federal Equalization Pro gram that Includes First Nations," *Policy Options*, May 16, 2018, https://policyoptions.irpp.org/magazines/may-2018/a-federal -equalization-program-that-includes-first-nations.

71 *Indigenous parliamentary ridings*: While this seems to me to be a reasonable extension of Canada's multinational principles, I recognize that my own views on Indigenous representation in Canada do not carry much authority. See, however, the argu ment developed by the pathbreaking Indigenous parliamentar ian Len Marchand in "Proportional Representation for Native Peoples," *Canadian Parliamentary Review* 13, no. 3 (1990): 9–10.

72 *"We are Treaty partners"*: Alvin Fiddler to Justin Trudeau, "Re: Preventable Deaths of Our Youth," January 18, 2017, http:// www.falconers.ca/wp-content/uploads/2017/01/Letter-to -Prime-Minister-Justin-Trudeau-Grand-Chief-Fiddler-January -17-2017.pdf. See also Tanya Talaga, *All Our Relations: Finding the Path Forward* (Toronto: House of Anansi Press, 2018).

72 *"reset"*: Tim Harper, "A Justin Trudeau Reset of First Nations Relations Aims Sky High: Harper," *Toronto Star*, December 9, 2015, https://www.thestar.com/news/canada/2015/12/09/a -justin-trudeau-reset-of-first-nations-relations-aims-sky-high -harper.html.

73 *"Mommy"*: A recording is available at https://www.youtube .com/watch?v=VZMauq1jszM&ab_channel=Jean-Philippe Boisbriand. The song was initially recorded as "Mommy Daddy" by Dominique Michel and Marc Gélinas.

74 *"There was much in it"*: George Orwell, *Homage to Catalonia* (Boston: Mariner Books, 1980 [1938]), 5.

75 *Fortuyn wrote and spoke explicitly*: Merijn Oudenampsen, *The Rise of the Dutch New Right: An Intellectual History of the Rightward Shift in Dutch Politics* (New York: Routledge, 2022).

75 *popular across all four official language groups*: Thomas Stephens, "Minaret Result Seen as 'Turning Point,'" SWI, November 29, 2009, https://www.swissinfo.ch/eng/minaret-result -seen-as—turning-point-/7793740.

CHAPTER 2: CONFEDERATION

77 *an annual parade*: André Alexis, *Days by Moonlight* (Toronto: Coach House Books, 2019), 70.

78 *"Men of the most exalted genius"*: John Adams, *Diary*, February 19, 1755, National Archives, Founders Online, https://founders .archives.gov/documents/Adams/01-01-02-0002-0002.

78 *"the love of fame"*: Alexander Hamilton, "Federalist 72," in Alexander Hamilton, James Madison, and John Jay, *The Federalist with Letters of "Brutus,"* ed. Terence Ball (Cambridge: Cambridge University Press, 2003 [1787]), 353.

78 *the Enlightenment theory*: Douglas Adair, "Fame and the Founding Fathers," in *Fame and the Founding Father: Essays* (Indianapolis: Liberty Fund, 1998 [1974]), 22–23.

79 *"political religion"*: Abraham Lincoln, "Address Before the Young Men's Lyceum of Springfield, Illinois: The Perpetuation of Our Political Institutions," in *Collected Works of Abraham Lincoln*, ed. Roy P. Basler et al. (New Brunswick, NJ: Rutgers University Press, 1953), 1:112.

79 *"Washington gave the child"* . . . *"The decorous relationship"* . . .

Notes

"His powerful will": Gore Vidal, *Burr* (New York: Vintage, 2011 [1973]), 50, 75, 119.

80 *"Thou shalt not"*: Exodus 20:4–5 (KJV).

81 *"A Canadian"*: Northrup Frye, "Letters in Canada: Poetry," in *Collected Works of Northrop Frye*, vol. 12: *Northrop Frye on Canada*, ed. Jean O'Grady and David Staines (Toronto: University of Toronto Press, 2003 [1953]), 106.

81 *"A French-Canadian"*: John Boyd, *Sir George-Étienne Cartier* (London, Macmillan, 1917), 159, quoted in Christopher Moore, *Three Weeks in Quebec City: The Meeting That Made Canada* (Toronto: Penguin Random House Canada, 2015).

82 *One long-standing interpretation*: Seymour Martin Lipset, *Continental Divide: The Values and Institutions of the United States and Canada* (New York: Routledge, 1990), 2. See also Russell J. Dalton, "Political Culture and Values," in *The United States and Canada: How Two Democracies Differ and Why It Matters*, ed., Paul J. Quirk (New York: Oxford University Press, 2019), 86–140.

84 *"flaunting the low"*: Pierre Ostiguy, "Populism: A Socio-Cultural Approach," in *The Oxford Handbook of Populism*, ed. Cristóbal Rovira Kaltwasser et al. (Oxford: Oxford University Press, 2017), 78.

84 *"will continue to enthusiastically support"*: Don Gonyea, "Today's GOP Is Donald Trump's Party," NPR, August 26, 2020, https://www.npr.org/2020/08/26/905803785/todays-gop-is-donald-trump-s-party.

85 *"I will tell you"*: Elizabeth Dias, "'Christianity Will Have Power,'" *New York Times*, August 9, 2020, https://www.nytimes.com/2020/08/09/us/evangelicals-trump-christianity.html.

85 *"And on the eighth day"*: Mike Allen, "Ron DeSantis' 'God Ad' Invokes God 10 Times in 96 Seconds," *Axios*, November 5, 2022,

https://www.axios.com/2022/11/05/ron-desantis-god-ad-florida
-governor.

86   *might turn to a powerful leader almost by default*: See Michael
     Freeden, *Ideologies and Political Theory: A Conceptual Approach*
     (Oxford: Oxford University Press, 1996), 76–77 and Nadia Ur-
     binati, *Me the People: How Populism Transforms Democracy*
     (Cambridge, MA: Harvard University Press, 2019), 163.

86   *"I alone can fix it"*: "Full Text: Donald Trump's 2016 Republican
     National Convention Speech," ABC News, July 22, 2016, https://
     abcnews.go.com/Politics/full-text-donald-trumps-2016-repub
     lican-national-convention/story?id=40786529.

86   *"men on horseback"* . . . *"It is at moments like the present"*:
     David A. Bell, *Men on Horseback: The Power of Charisma in
     the Age of Revolution* (New York: Farrar, Straus and Giroux,
     2020), 12.

87   *"Something of the same kind"*: John Adams to Benjamin Rush,
     March 19, 1812, National Archives, Founders Online, https://
     founders.archives.gov/documents/Adams/99-02-02-5768;
     quoted in Bell, *Men on Horseback*, 75.

87   *dug up Bolívar's bones*: "Venezuela's Chavez Exhumes Hero
     Simon Bolivar's Bones," BBC News, July 17, 2010, https://
     www.bbc.com/news/world-latin-america-10669051.

89   *"What the Stuarts had tried to do"*: *District of Columbia v.
     Heller*, 554 U.S. 570 (2008), 21.

89   *an especially exalted form of address*: For example, Kamala Har-
     ris's tweet on being announced as Joe Biden's running mate: "I'm
     honored to join him as our party's nominee for Vice President,
     and do what it takes to make him our Commander-in-Chief" (Ka-
     mala Harris [@KamalaHarris], August 11, 2020, 4:56 p.m., Twit-
     ter, twitter.com/kamalaharris/status/1293290197103390721.

Notes

89 *forcibly casting out demons*: For example, Mark 9:25, Matthew 8:32, Luke 4:35.

90 *paths not taken*: H. W. Brands, *The First American: The Life and Times of Benjamin Franklin* (New York: Anchor 2002 [2000]), 239; "Franklin's Notes for a Conversation with Lord Chatham," January 31, 1775, National Archives, Founders Online, https://founders.archives.gov/documents/Franklin/01-21-02-0251.

90 *"peaceable kingdom"*: See J. A. Frank, Michael J. Kelly, and Thomas H. Mitchell, "The Myth of the Peaceable Kingdom: Interpretations of Violence in Canadian History," *Peace Research* 15, no. 3 (1983): 52–60.

91 *Democracy and independence*: The American colonies also had elected assemblies that predated independence, but their subversion by the Crown was one of the main grievances of the Revolution, so that the causes of domestic self-government and separation from Britain became closely entangled.

91 *"Without political liberty"*: Louis-Hippolyte LaFontaine, "Address to the Electors of Terrebonne," *L'Aurore des Canadas*, August 28, 1840, trans. John Ralston Saul. I am indebted to Saul's discussion of the "Address" in his *A Fair Country: Telling Truths about Canada* (Toronto: Penguin Canada, 2008), 130–34.

92 *"was an executive councillor"*: This is a description of William Allen, a member of the Family Compact. H. G. J. Aitken, "The Family Compact and the Welland Canal Company," *Canadian Journal of Economics and Political Science* 17 (1952): 76.

93 *"the well-being promised us"* . . . *"efficient participation"*: Louis-Hippolyte LaFontaine, "Address to the Electors of Terrebonne," August 28, 1840, trans. William F. Maton, Solon Law Archive, http://www.solon.org/Constitutions/Canada

/English/PreConfederation/The_Address_to_the_Electors_of
_Terrebonne_1840.html.

94 *the king could still fire the prime minister*: The last royal favourite to serve as British prime minister was John Stuart, the Earl of
Bute, in 1762; the last prime minister to be sacked by the monarch was William Lamb, Viscount Melbourne, in 1834.

94 *the colony's first fully responsible government*: Two months earlier, reformers led by Joseph Howe secured responsible government in Nova Scotia, the first in the provinces that would
become Canada.

95 *"railroad boom"*: Moore, *Three Weeks in Quebec City*, 22.

95 *The Canadian oligarchs*: This argument is developed in Doug
Saunders, *Maximum Canada: Why 35 Million Canadians Are
Not Enough* (Toronto: Knopf Canada, 2017).

96 *"the goal essential to our prosperity"*: LaFontaine, "Address to
the Electors of Terrebonne," trans. Saul.

97 *"What astonishing changes"* . . . *"From the high ground"*: George
Washington to John Jay, August 1, 1786, May 18, 1786, in *The
Writings of George Washington from the Original Manuscript
Sources*, ed. John C. Fitzpatrick (Washington, DC: US Govern-
ment Printing Office, 1931–1944), 28:503, 28:431–2. The capital-
ization follows the original.

97 *"devouring each other"*: Benjamin Rush to David Ramsay [Mar.
or Apr. 1788], in *Letters of Benjamin Rush*, ed. L. H. Butterneld
(Princeton, NJ: Princeton University Press, 1951), 1:454.

97 *"men of narrow souls"*: George Clymer, quoted in Jerry Grund-
fest, *George Clymer: Philadelphia Revolutionary, 1739–1813*
(New York: Arno Press, 1982), 165.

97 *"a particular interest"* . . . *"crudeness"*: James Madison to Edmund Pendleton, January 9, 1787, and to George Washington,

December 24, 1786, in *The Papers of James Madison*, ed. William T. Hutchinson et al. (Charlottesville: University of Virginia Press, 1975), 9:244, 9:225. The quotations in this paragraph are all cited in Gordon S. Wood, "Interests and Disinterestedness in the Making of the Constitution," in *Beyond Confederation*, ed. Richard Beeman, Stephen Botein, and Edward C. Carter II (Chapel Hill: University of North Carolina Press, 1987), 71, 76, 74.

97   *"astonish our small souls"*: Montesquieu, *The Spirit of the Laws*, ed. Anne M. Cohler et al. (Cambridge: Cambridge University Press, 1989 [1748]), 35.

98   *"we cannot quite imagine"*: Wood, "Interests and Disinterestedness," 84.

99   *"a rage for paper money"*: James Madison, "Federalist 10," in *The Federalist*, 46.

100 *"with our despairing effort"*: Wood, "Interests and Disinterestedness," 81–82.

100 *"a new Nationality"*: Charles Monck, January 19, 1865, quoted in Peter B. Waite, "Introduction to the First Edition," *The Confederation Debates in the Province of Canada, 1865*, 2nd ed., ed. P. B. Waite (Montreal: McGill-Queen's University Press, 2006), xl.

101 *premodern understanding of* party: See Harvey C. Mansfield, *Statesmanship and Party Government: A Study of Burke and Bolingbroke* (Chicago: University of Chicago Press, 1965).

101 *"Politicians are generally cunning fellows"*: Edward Whelan, *The Union of the British Provinces* (Summerside, PEI: Pioneer Publishing, 1949 [1865]), 109 (cited in Moore, *Three Weeks in Quebec City*, 111).

102 *a sign of public support*: *Toronto Globe*, March 13, 1865, quoted

Notes

in Ged Martin, "Introduction to the 2006 Edition," Waite, ed., *The Confederation Debates*, xxvi.

103 *the public debates on Confederation*: Martin, "Introduction to the 2006 Edition," xxiii.

104 *"bitterness and virulence"*: Richard Cartwright, Province of Canada, Legislature, *Parliamentary Debates on the Subject of the Confederation of the British North American Provinces*, 1865, p. 821 (cited in Waite, "Introduction to the First Edition," xli).

105 *"Constitutional Democrats"*: Robert A. Caro, *The Years of Lyndon Johnson*, vol. 3, *Master of the Senate* (New York: Vintage, 2003), 220.

105 *"glorious liberty document"*: Frederick Douglass, "What to the Slave Is the Fourth of July?," in *The Speeches of Frederick Douglass*, ed. John R. McKivigan, Julie Husband, and Heather L. Kaufman (New Haven, CT: Yale University Press, 2018 [1852]), 88. See also Rob Goodman, "Slavery and Oratory: Frederick Douglass in the History of Rhetoric," *American Political Science Review* (online first), February 10, 2023, https://doi.org/10.1017/S0003055423000011.

107 *"we would be forced"*: Étienne-Paschal Taché, February 3, 1865, in Waite, ed., *The Confederation Debates*, 1.

107 *"Events stronger than advocacy"*: Thomas D'Arcy McGee, February 9, 1865, in Waite, ed., *The Confederation Debates*, 55.

108 *"If the federated provinces"*: Moore, *Three Weeks in Quebec City*, 132.

109 *"to describe the predicament"*: Quentin Skinner, *Liberty before Liberalism* (Cambridge: Cambridge University Press, 1998), 42.

109 *"The height of misery"*: Orlando Patterson, *Slavery and Social Death: A Comparative Study* (Cambridge, MA: Harvard University Press, 1982), 77.

Notes

112 *"towering genius"* . . . *"It sees no distinction"* . . . *"That we re-mained free"*: Lincoln, "Address Before the Young Men's Lyceum," 114–15.

116 *"managed a century and a half"*: Juan J. Linz, "The Perils of Presidentialism," *Journal of Democracy* 1, no. 1 (1990): 52.

116 *They set up parliaments*: Ezra Klein, *Why We're Polarized* (New York: Simon & Schuster, 2020), 202.

116 *"Our parliamentary and judicial institutions"*: George Grant, *Lament for a Nation: The Defeat of Canadian Nationalism* (Montreal: McGill-Queens University Press, 2005 [1965]), 72.

117 *"all the personal privileges"*: Jean Louis de Lolme, *The Constitution of England*, ed. David Lieberman (Indianapolis: Liberty Fund, 2007 [1771]), 143.

117 *"fixed unassailable point"*: Benjamin Constant, *Principles of Politics Applicable to All Representative Governments*, in *Political Writings*, ed. Biancamaria Fontana (Cambridge: Cambridge University Press, 1988 [1815]), 190. This and the passage from de Lolme are cited in William Selinger, *Parliamentarism: From Burke to Weber* (Cambridge: Cambridge University Press, 2019), 43, 131.

118 *"picture of the corner grocer"*: For various attributions of this line (and for some objections to it), see Alisa Luxenberg, "Further Light on the Critical Reception of Goya's 'Family of Charles IV' as Caricature," *Artibus et Historiae* 23, no. 46 (2002): 179.

120 *"is forced to hear"* . . . *"its magnitude and melodrama"*: Walter Bagehot, *The English Constitution*, 2nd ed. (London: Chapman & Hall, 1873), 53–54.

120 *institutionalizing an official opposition*: See Jeremy Waldron, *Political Political Theory: Essays on Institutions* (Cambridge, MA: Harvard University Press, 2016).

Notes

123 *nearly quadrupling its size*: Peter H. Russell, *Canada's Odyssey: A Country Based on Incomplete Conquests* (Toronto: University of Toronto Press, 2017), 317.

123 *Across the world, parliamentary systems*: See, for example, Lauri Karvonen, *The Personalisation of Politics: A Study of Parliamentary Democracies* (Colchester, UK: ECPR Press, 2009).

124 *Scott Morrison's government*: Andrew Probyn and Jake Evans, "Anthony Albanese Orders Probe into Claims of Scott Morrison's Secret Ministry Grab during COVID-19," ABC News, August 14, 2022, https://www.abc.net.au/news/2022-08-15/scott-morrison-secret-ministry-appointments-to-be-investi gated/101332916.

124 *a government of exceptional centralization*: See Paul Wells, "The Obvious Lesson Justin Trudeau Keeps Failing to Learn," *Maclean's*, July 29, 2020, https://www.macleans.ca/politics/ottawa/the-obvious-lessons-justin-trudeau-keeps-failing-to-learn.

125 *"running for prime minister"*: Darren Major, "Pierre Poilievre Becomes First MP to Bid for Conservative Party Leadership," CBC News, February 5, 2022, www.cbc.ca/news/politics/pierre-poil ievre-running-for-conservative-leadership-1.6341335.

125 *falsely described*: Stephanie Levitz and Alex Ballingall, "Pierre Poilievre Slams Justin Trudeau's 'Radical Woke Coalition' As Return to Parliament Looms," *Toronto Star*, September 12, 2022, https://www.thestar.com/politics/federal/2022/09/12/pierre -poilievre-pledges-to-restore-hope-to-canadians-in-inaugural -address-to-mps.html.

125 *hidden orders-in-council*: Elizabeth Thompson, "Trudeau Government Has Adopted Dozens of Secret Cabinet Orders Since Coming to Power," CBC News, June 1, 2022, https://www.cbc .ca/news/politics/secret-orders-in-council-1.6467450.

Notes

125 *mass shooting inquiry*: Haley Ryan, "2nd RCMP Staffer Suggests Commissioner under Political Pressure after N.S. Mass Shooting," CBC News, June 28, 2022, https://www.cbc.ca/news/canada/nova-scotia/2nd-rcmp-staffer-suggests-commissioner-under-political-pressure-after-n-s-mass-shooting-1.6504330.

126 *"They've been following you"*: Pierre Poilievre (@PierrePoilievre), May 6, 2022, 11:50 a.m., Twitter, https://twitter.com/PierrePoilievre/status/1522604660762230787.

126 *"actually talking about"*: Tyler Clark, "Ontario Party Leader Derek Sloan Talks 'Freedoms' in Sudbury," *Sudbury.com*, May 9, 2022, https://www.sudbury.com/local-news/ontario-party-leader-derek-sloan-talks-freedoms-in-sudbury-5345587.

126 *"A FUTURE WORLD GOVERNMENT"*: Maxime Bernier (@MaximeBernier), January 8, 2019, 9:04 p.m. Twitter, https://twitter.com/MaximeBernier/status/1082820465725452288. On the quotations in this paragraph, see Andrew Coyne, "The Vacuum at the Centre of Canadian Politics," *Globe and Mail*, June 24, 2022, https://www.theglobeandmail.com/opinion/article-the-vacuum-at-the-centre-of-canadian-politics-an-incompetent-unethical, and "The Paranoid Style in Conservative Politics Has Deep Roots," *Globe and Mail*, May 26, 2022, https://www.theglobeandmail.com/opinion/article-the-paranoid-style-in-conservative-politics-has-deep-roots.

127 *citizen assemblies*: See, for example, Arash Abizadeh, "Let's Replace Canada's Senate with a Randomly Selected Citizen Assembly," *Montreal Gazette*, December 7, 2016, https://montrealgazette.com/opinion/columnists/opinion-lets-replace-canadas-senate-with-a-randomly-selected-citizen-assembly; Simone Chambers and Patti Tamara Lenard, "Reflections on the Democratic Deficit in Canada and the United States," in *Imperfect*

Democracies: The Democratic Deficit in Canada and the United States, ed. Patt Tamara Lenard and Richard Simeon (Vancouver: University of British Columbia Press, 2015), 322–26; Amy Lang and Mark E. Warren, "Supplementary Democracy? Democratic Deficits and Citizens' Assemblies," in *Imperfect Democracies*, ed. Lenard and Simeon, 291–314; and Hélène Landemore, *Open Democracy: Reinventing Popular Rule for the Twenty-First Century* (Princeton, NJ: Princeton University Press, 2020).

CHAPTER 3: SOLIDARITY

132 *ban or restrict the teaching of "divisive concepts"*: For a comprehensive list, see "PEN America Index of Educational Gag Orders," PEN America, n.d., docs.google.com/spreadsheets/d/1Tj5WQVBmB6SQg-zP_M8uZsQQGH09Txm BY73v23zpyr0/edit#gid=267763711.

133 *the largest demonstrations*: Larry Buchanan, Quoctrung Bui, and Jugal K. Patel, "Black Lives Matter May Be the Largest Movement in U.S. History," *New York Times*, July 3, 2020, https://www.nytimes.com/interactive/2020/07/03/us/george-floyd-protests-crowd-size.html.

133 *"our kids to hate America"*: "Cotton, McConnell, Colleagues Introduce Bill to Defund 1619 Project Curriculum," Office of Senator Tom Cotton, June 14, 2021, https://www.cotton.senate.gov/news/press-releases/cotton-mcconnell-colleagues-introduce-bill-to-defund-1619-project-curriculum.

133 *" 'Critical race theory' "* . . . *"Strung together"*: Benjamin Wallace-Wells, "How a Conservative Activist Invented the Conflict over Critical Race Theory," *The New Yorker*, June 18, 2021, https://www.newyorker.com/news/annals-of-inquiry

/how-a-conservative-activist-invented-the-conflict-over-criti
cal-race-theory.

133 *"The goal"*: Christopher Rufo (@realchrisrufo), March 15, 2021, 3:17 p.m., Twitter, https://twitter.com/realchrisrufo/sta tus/1371541044592996352.

134 *"(5) The 1619 Project"*: S. 4292, "To Prohibit Federal Funds from Being Made Available to Teach the 1619 Project Curriculum in Elementary Schools and Secondary schools, and for Other Purposes," July 23, 2020, https://www.govinfo.gov/content/pkg /BILLS-116s4292is/html/BILLS-116s4292is.htm.

138 *"drove such a wedge"*: W. E. B. Du Bois, *Black Reconstruction in America* (New Brunswick, NJ: Transaction, 2013 [1935]), 700. See also David R. Roediger, *The Wages of Whiteness: Race and the Making of the American Working Class* (New York: Verso, 1991); Joshua Zeitz, "Does the White Working Class Really Vote against Its Own Interests?," *Politico Magazine*, December 31, 2017, https://www.politico.com/magazine/story/2017/12/31 /trump-white-working-class-history-216200.

138 *"When his undernourished children"*: Martin Luther King Jr., "Address at the Conclusion of the Selma to Montgomery March," in *A Call to Conscience: The Landmark Speeches of Dr. Martin Luther King, Jr.*, ed. Clayborne Carson and Kris Shepard (New York: Warner Books, 2001 [1965]), 124.

139 *"You start out"*: Rick Perlstein, "Exclusive: Lee Atwater's Infamous 1981 Interview on the Southern Strategy," *The Nation*, November 13, 2012, https://www.thenation.com/article/archive/exclu sive-lee-atwaters-infamous-1981-interview-southern-strategy.

141 *"a treaty between"*: Toronto Metropolitan University, "Land Acknowledgment," n.d., http://www.torontomu.ca/aec/land -acknowledgment.

Notes

142 *"I started to see"*: " 'I Regret It': Hayden King on Writing Ryerson University's Territorial Acknowledgement," CBC Radio, January 18, 2019, https://www.cbc.ca/radio/unreserved/redrawing-the-lines-1.4973363/i-regret-it-hayden-king-on-writing-ryerson-university-s-territorial-acknowledgement-1.4973371.

142 *more than twice as likely*: " 'We Do Not Accept Your Apology,' Activist Tells Toronto's Police Chief after Race-Based Data Released," CBC News, June 15, 2022, https://www.cbc.ca/news/canada/toronto/toronto-police-race-based-data-use-force-strip-searches-1.6489151.

142 *a third of all the people*: Darren Major, "Indigenous Women Make Up Almost Half the Female Prison Population, Ombudsman Says," CBC News, December 18, 2021, https://www.cbc.ca/news/politics/indigenous-women-half-inmate-population-canada-1.6289674.

143 *Western alienation*: See David McGrane, "Western Alienation or Mere Critique of Federal Government Policies?: Saskatchewan Social Democrats' View of Federalism from 1900 to Present," *International Journal of Canadian Studies* 32 (2005): 205–35.

145 *"When American friends"*: Wade Davis, "The Unraveling of America," *Rolling Stone*, August 6, 2020, https://www.rollingstone.com/politics/political-commentary/covid-19-end-of-american-era-wade-davis-1038206.

147 *an average of 884 people*: Rob Ferguson, "Leaked Report Shows Soaring Number of Patients Waiting in Ontario Hospital Emergency Rooms," *Toronto Star*, October 12, 2022, https://www.thestar.com/politics/provincial/2022/10/12/leaked-report-shows-soaring-number-of-patients-waiting-in-ontario-hospital-emergency-rooms.html.

147 *"presumably due to interminable wait times"*: Alan Drummond,

Notes

"State of Emergency: Inside Canada's ER Crisis," *Maclean's*, November 10, 2022, https://www.macleans.ca/longforms/er-doctor -healthcare-crisis-canada.

147 *"are full of tension"*: Ibid.

147 *gap between house prices and incomes*: Deena Zaidi, "How Canada Has Taken On More Mortgage Debt Than Any Other G7 Nation, Explained in 5 Charts," CTV News, November 13, 2022, https://www.ctvnews.ca/business/how-canada-has -taken-on-more-mortgage-debt-than-any-other-g7-nation-ex plained-in-5-charts-1.6149517.

147 *our housing supply*: Amy Legate-Wolf, "Canadian Housing Now the Worst in Affordability among G7 Countries," Yahoo Finance, July 7, 2022, https://ca.finance.yahoo.com/news/cana dian-housing-now-worst-affordability-203000416.html.

147 *least affordable cities*: Joanne Lee-Young, "Vancouver Is the Third Least-Affordable City in the World: Survey," *Vancouver Sun*, April 19, 2022, https://vancouversun.com/news/local -news/vancouver-third-least-affordable-city-demographia.

148 *selling your time*: See Martin Hägglund, *This Life: Secular Faith and Spiritual Freedom* (New York: Penguin Random House, 2020).

148 *a ravenous appetite for our time*: As Jeremiah Moss, a housing reporter, put it, "Low rent allows so much to happen. It allows people to take risks. . . . It means time and it means you can fail and survive." See Robin Grearson, "The Aesthetics of Gentrification, and New York's Top-Down Approach to Change," *Hyperallergic*, May 9, 2018, https://hyperallergic.com/440547 /the-aesthetics-of-gentrification-and-new-yorks-top-down-ap proach-to-change.

150 *"generational injustice"*: Leyland Cecco, "Spiraling Housing

233

Prices Are a 'Generational Injustice,' Says Canada's Deputy PM," *The Guardian*, April 12, 2022, https://www.theguardian .com/world/2022/apr/12/canada-housing-prices-chrystia-free land.

150 *"big-city gatekeepers"*: "Poilievre Calls Out 'Gatekeepers' While Addressing Home Ownership in Vancouver," YouTube video, posted by "Western Standard," April 11, 2022, https://www .youtube.com/watch?v=TkVldVJ_C-s.

152 *"Canada is free"*: Pierre Poilievre (@PierrePoilievre), June 18, 2022, 12:33 p.m., Twitter, https://twitter.com/pierrepoilievre /status/1538198329053487104.

153 *"It is only mildly amusing"*: Edward Luttwak, "Why Fascism Is the Wave of the Future," *London Review of Books*, April 7, 1994, https://www.lrb.co.uk/the-paper/v16/n07/edward-luttwak /why-fascism-is-the-wave-of-the-future.

155 *"Never has such a torrent"*: Adapted from George Grant, *Lament for a Nation: The Defeat of Canadian Nationalism* (Montreal: McGill-Queens University Press, 2005 [1965]), 3.

157 *"inchoate desire to build"*: Ibid., 68–69.

158 *"Capitalism is, after all"*: Ibid., 46–47.

159 *"Nationalism had to go"* . . . *"The impossibility of conservatism"*: Ibid., 16, 67.

159 *Grant won a following*: Andrew Potter, "Introduction to the 40th Anniversary Edition," in Ibid., xxxi.

160 *"big tech"* . . . *"woke capital"*: Timothy Noah, "Prepare for a New Republican War on 'Woke' Capital," *New Republic*, November 9, 2022, https://newrepublic.com/article/168607/re publican-majority-war-woke-capital.

160 *"the reigning political consensus"* . . . *"closer and closer"*: "Senator Josh Hawley's Speech at the National Conservatism Con-

ference," Office of Senator Josh Hawley, July 18, 2019, https://www.hawley.senate.gov/senator-josh-hawleys-speech-national-conservatism-conference.

160 *"somewheres"*: Aaron Wherry, "Where You Live Is Who You Are: Erin O'Toole and the New Culture War," CBC News, December 4, 2020, https://www.cbc.ca/news/politics/erin-otoole-culture-war-pandemic-statues-immigration-1.5826976.

161 *"confidently declare[s]"*: Viktor Orbán, "Prime Minister Viktor Orbán's Speech at the 29th Bálványos Summer Open University and Student Camp," July 28, 2018, https://2015-2022.miniszterelnok.hu/prime-minister-viktor-orbans-speech-at-the-29th-balvanyos-summer-open-university-and-student-camp.

161 *capitalism is the universal solvent*: Ironically, the right is indebted for this insight to Marx and Engels, who observed in 1848 that under the revolutionary forces released by capitalism, "all that is solid melts into air, all that is holy is profaned." See Karl Marx and Friedrich Engels, "The Communist Manifesto," in *Karl Marx: Selected Writings*, ed. Lawrence H. Simon (Indianapolis: Hackett, 1994), 161–62.

161 *"In a liberal system"*: Viktor Orbán, "Orbán's Full Speech at Tusványos," *Visegrád Post*, July 29, 2019, https://visegradpost.com/en/2019/07/29/orbans-full-speech-at-tusvanyos-political-philosophy-upcoming-crisis-and-projects-for-the-next-15-years.

161 *"perfect consumer slaves"*: David Corn, "How Giorgia Meloni's Win in Italy Helps Us Understand a US Senate Race," *Mother Jones*, October 4, 2022, https://www.motherjones.com/politics/2022/10/how-giorgia-melonis-win-in-italy-helps-us-understand-a-us-senate-race.

163 *"manhood" for Hawley*: "Senator Hawley Delivers National Conservatism Keynote on the Left's Attack on Men in

America," Office of Senator Josh Hawley, November 1, 2021, https://www.hawley.senate.gov/senator-hawley-delivers-national-conservatism-keynote-lefts-attack-men-america.

163 *"This is why we"*: "Speech by Prime Minister Viktor Orbán at the 31st Bálványos Summer Free University and Student Camp," About Hungary, July 23, 2022, https://abouthungary.hu/speeches-and-remarks/speech-by-prime-minister-viktor-orban-at-the-31-st-balvanyos-summer-free-university-and-student-camp.

164 herrenvolk *(or "master race") democracy*: The term was coined by Pierre L. van den Berghe, *Race and Racism: A Comparative Perspective* (New York: Wiley, 1967). See also Justin C. Mueller, "America's Herrenvolk Democracy Is a Social Democracy for the White Majority," *Milwaukee Independent*, November 3, 2017, https://www.milwaukeeindependent.com/articles/americas-herrenvolk-democracy-social-democracy-white-majority.

164 *"We must make every effort"*: Hawley, "The Left's Attack on Men in America."

164 *"I'm the guy pushing"*: Daniella Diaz, "Bannon: 'Darkness Is Good,'" CNN, November 18, 2016, https://www.cnn.com/2016/11/18/politics/steve-bannon-donald-trump-hollywood-reporter-interview.

164 *deliberate exclusion of most Black workers*: Ira Katznelson, *Fear Itself: The New Deal and the Origins of Our Times* (New York: W. W. Norton, 2013).

165 *lowest ebb of approval*: See "How Popular Is Donald Trump?," *FiveThirtyEight*, January 20, 2021, https://projects.fivethirtyeight.com/trump-approval-ratings. A number of pundits, including Matthew Yglesias, have pointed out the low point of Trump's popularity coincided with the 2017 tax cut bill. See Matthew

Yglesias, "Trump's Biggest Political Weakness Is on Regular Policy Issues," *Vox*, January 18, 2018, https://www.vox.com/policy -and-politics/2018/1/18/16899734/trump-weakness-policy.

165 *long-standing networks*: See Theda Skocpol and Vanessa Williamson, *The Tea Party and the Remaking of Republican Conservatism* (New York: Oxford University Press, 2012).

169 *"moral self-recognition"* . . . *"structures of feeling"*: Mike Davis, *Old Gods, New Enigmas: Marx's Lost Theory* (New York: Verso, 2018), 146. Thanks to Terence Renaud for calling my attention to this passage (https://twitter.com/terry_renaud/sta tus/1568243295054086144).

170 *"Is it possible"*: Du Bois, "Of Mr. Booker T. Washington and Others," in *The Souls of Black Folk* (Oxford: Oxford University Press, 2007 [1903]), 39.

170 *"Let the Negro once understand"*: Du Bois, *Black Reconstruction*, 297.

170 *"Without political liberty"*: Louis-Hippolyte LaFountaine, "Address to the Electors of Terrebonne," *L'Aurore des Canadas*, August 28, 1840, trans. John Ralston Saul.

CHAPTER 4: POWER

171 *"a little adjacent"*: Al Purdy, "The Country North of Belleville," quoted in Margaret Atwood, *Survival: A Thematic Guide to Canadian Literature* (Toronto: House of Anansi Press, 2012 [1972]), 118.

172 *"a total and complete shutdown"*: Jessica Taylor, "Trump Calls for 'Total and Complete Shutdown of Muslims Entering' U.S.," NPR, December 7, 2015, https://www.npr .org/2015/12/07/458836388/trump-calls-for-total-and-com plete-shutdown-of-muslims-entering-u-s.

Notes

172 *"exuberant Canadians"* . . . *"There is no relationship"*: Michael Paulson, "Justin Trudeau Brings Ivanka Trump to Broadway Show on Welcoming Outsiders," *New York Times*, March 15, 2017, https://www.nytimes.com/2017/03/15/theater/justin-trudeau-ivanka-trump-broadway-come-from-away.html. At the time of the performance, Ivanka Trump was still an informal advisor to her father, but she was officially appointed to the role of presidential advisor by the end of the month.

174 *"buy back the country"*: Garth Stevenson, "The Third Option," *International Journal* 33, no. 2 (1978): 431.

175 *"Anglo Canadian Culture"*: Callum Wratten, "Anglo Canadian Culture Revealed Just to Be a Series of Brand Loyalties," *The Beaverton*, July 12, 2018, https://www.thebeaverton.com/2018/07/study-anglo-canadian-culture-revealed-just-to-be-a-series-of-brand-loyalties.

175 *settlement patterns of Upper Canada*: Doug Saunders discusses the economic motivations of the Upper Canada Rebellion in *Maximum Canada: Why 35 Million Canadians Are Not Enough* (Toronto: Knopf Canada, 2017), 10–19.

176 *"If everyone was broadly aware"*: David Graeber and David Wengrow, *The Dawn of Everything: A New History of Humanity* (Farrar, Straus and Giroux, 2021), 174 (emphasis added).

177 *"Societies live by borrowing"*: Nathan Schlanger, *Marcel Mauss: Techniques, Technology, and Civilization* (New York: Durkheim Press/Berghahn Books, 2006), 44.

178 *"almost a parody"*: John Hancock, "The Third Option: An Idea Whose Time Has Finally Come?" *International Journal* 70, no. 2 (2015): 329.

178 *"reduce the present Canadian vulnerability"*: Mitchell Sharp,

Notes

"Canada–U.S. Relations: Options for the Future," *International Perspectives*, special issue (Autumn 1972): 18.

179 *"It is time"*: Richard Nixon, "Address to a Joint Meeting of the Canadian Parliament," Ottawa, April 14, 1972, https://www.presidency.ucsb.edu/documents/address-joint-meeting-the-canadian-parliament.

179 *"the special relationship"*: Mitchell Sharp, "Canada's Trading Revolution," O. D. Skelton Memorial Lecture, 1995, https://www.international.gc.ca/gac-amc/programs-programmes/od_skelton/mitchell_sharp_lecture-conference.aspx?lang=eng.

180 *that assumption no longer held*: Ibid.

180 *"far-reaching policies"*: Hancock, "The Third Option," 330.

180 *"Geography . . . subjects Canadians"*: Sharp, "Canada's Trading Revolution."

181 *"the more extreme kinds"*: Sharp, *Which Reminds Me . . . A Memoir* (Toronto: University of Toronto Press, 1994), 186 (quoted in Hancock, "The Third Option," 330).

181 *"lessen the vulnerability"*: Mitchell Sharp, "Canada–U.S. Relations," 17.

181 *largely toothless*: Stevenson, "The Third Option," 428; see also John Ralston Saul, *A Fair Country: Telling Truths about Canada* (Toronto: Penguin Canada, 2008), 215.

181 *the private sector disagreed*: See Gordon Mace and Gérard Hervouet, "Canada's Third Option: A Complete Failure?" *Canadian Public Policy/Analyse de Politiques* 15, no. 4 (1989): 387–404.

184 *gradually trending downwards*: Hancock, "The Third Option," 337; Kip Beckman, "What Might Canada's Future Exports Look Like?," Conference Board of Canada, publication 13–21, November 16, 2012, https://www.canada2030.ca/wp-content/uploads/2013/08/CBoardC_CanadasFutureExports_BR.pdf.

Notes

188 *"The beneficial effect"*: Ursula K. Le Guin, *Always Coming Home* (Berkeley: University of California Press, 2001 [1985]), 473.

189 *immigration activists renewed*: Zainab Abu Alrob and John Shields, "The Safe Third Country Agreement, Irregular Migration, and Refugee Rights: A Canadian Policy Challenge," Ryerson University, March 2020, https://bmrc-irmu.info.yorku.ca /files/2020/03/Asylum-Seekers-Safe-Third-Country-Resilience -Final-March-2020.pdf. Challenges to the agreement date back to 2005, the year after it went into effect.

191 *"legislation restricting freedom of speech"*: Eric J. Evans, *William Pitt the Younger* (London: Routledge, 1999), 57.

192 *"Every man is surrounded"*: Jane Austen, *Northanger Abbey* (Cambridge: Cambridge University Press 2006 [1817]), 203.

192 *"We will not desert our Fatherland"*: See Hans Kundnani, "Can Germany's Social Democrats Offer an Alternative?," *Dissent*, Fall 2013, http://www.dissentmagazine.org/article/can-germanys -social-democrats-offer-an-alternative.

193 *Derrick Bell famously and controversially argued*: Derrick A. Bell Jr., "*Brown v. Board of Education* and the Interest-Convergence Dilemma," *Harvard Law Review* 93, no. 3 (1980): 518–33.

193 *a reaction to out-of-control Western liberalism*: N. S. Lyons, "The Triumph and Terror of Wang Huning," *Palladium*, October 11, 2021, https://palladiummag.com/2021/10/11/the-triumph -and-terror-of-wang-huning.

193 *"Do we really want"*: "Putin's Speech on Annexation: What Exactly Did He Say," Al Jazeera, September 30, 2022, https://www .aljazeera.com/news/2022/9/30/russia-ukraine-war-putins-annex ation-speech-what-did-he-say.

CONCLUSION: HERE

199 *"imagined communities"*: Benedict Anderson, *Imagined Communities: Reflections on the Origin and Spread of Nationalism* (New York: Verso, 2016 [1983]).

200 Where is here?: Northrop Frye, "Conclusion to a Literary History of Canada," in *The Bush Garden: Essays on the Canadian Imagination* (Toronto: House of Anansi Press, 2017 [1971]), 542.

Index

absorption, fear of, 10, 17–18
Adams, John, 87
"Address to the Electors
    of Terrebonne"
    (LaFontaine), 91
Alabama, 38
Alexis, André, 77
Algonquin Provincial Park,
    197–198
alliances, 172–173, 189–191
American South, 62–63, 137
anti-Americanism, 178–188
anticapitalism, 158–160
anti-immigration, 53–56,
    74–76
anti-vax movement, 15–16
Atwater, Lee, 139n
Atwood, Margaret, 7, 8
Austen, Jane, 192
Australia, 54, 124

authoritarianism, 17
    in America, 23
    charismatic, 110
    foundation of, 84
    and Indigenous
        reconciliation, 70
    populist, 85–87
    shock as weapon of, 23–24
    violence of, 40

Bagehot, Walter, 120, 121
Baldwin, Robert, 94–96
Bannon, Steve, 15, 164
Beaverton, The, 175
Bell, David A., 86, 87
Bell, Derrick, 193
Bernier, Maxime, 46, 126
Biden, Joe, 41–43, 99, 190
Bill 21, 74, 75, 104
Bill 96, 72, 75–76

Index

Index

Index

Ocasio-Cortez, Alexandria, 67
Ohio, 38
Ontario, 127, 147
Orbán, Viktor, 160–161, 163
Orbánism, 84–85
Orwell, George, 34–35, 74
Ostiguy, Pierre, 84
O'Toole, Erin, 160, 163
Ottawa blockade, 12, 13, 15,
    45–46, 70, 158

Packer, George, 66
parliamentarism, 113–127
    in Britain, 93–94
    in Canada, 95, 102–103,
        113–127
    flexibility of, 127
    as government by
        discussion, 119–123, 127
    innovations transforming,
        114
    as newer than American
        system, 113–115
    and political charisma,
        117–119, 122
    in post-war restructurings,
        116
    responsiveness to voters in,
        115–116
    threats to, 123–127
    visual language of,
        113–114
Parti Rouge, 101
PBS, 21

"people, the"
    American membership in, 47
    broad concept of, 85–86
    and Canada as
        multinational country, 18,
        19, 30, 46–47
    in democracies, 30–32
    in dominant Canadian
        historical perspective, 49
    idea of Real People vs.,
        29–30
    language used about, 33–35
    struggle over makeup of, 45
    and voting rights, 32–34
Pitt, William, 90
Poilievre, Pierre, 54, 125, 126,
    150–152
polarization
    over democracy in America,
        46
    worldwide, 191
political change model, 83, 96
political culture
    American, 65–67, 111–113
    and Canada's Third Option,
        182–186
    Canadian, 90–96, 108–109,
        111, 166–167, 182–183
    in presidential systems,
        119–120
political debates, 119–123
political institutions
    American, 38–39, 116
    Canadian, 116

253

political violence, 39–40, 88–89
politics, 8–9
    American, 8, 11, 36–37,
      45, 65–67, 99, 136, 137,
      165–166
    American model of, 90
    of American southern
      nationalism, 64
    Canadian, 13, 17–18, 45,
      53–59, 66–67, 101–104,
      150, 176
    coherence in, 154–155
    conspiracy theories in, 111
    election denial, 35–36
    of Europeans, 8
    fair shares in, 32
    of grief, 58–59
    idea of "the people" in,
      31–34
    of middle and lesser
      powers, 196
    Real People Principle in,
      29–30, 36, 45
    reigning consensus in,
      160–161
    revolutionary vs. ordinary,
      83
    right-populist, 137
    Third Option, 180, 186–188
    thorniest questions in, 132
    see also specific issues
populism, 84–86
    in Canada, 45–46, 70, 75
    enduring dynamics of, 156

and immigration, 54, 74, 75
in multinational
    democracies, 74
power, 171–196
    American, Canada's
      relationship with,
      189– 191
    and Canada's Third Option,
      178–186
    concentration of, in early
      Canada, 92–93
    conferred by Real People
      Principle, 83–84
    and constructive
      dishonesties in alliances,
      172–173
    economic, 151, 170
    and economic integration,
      174–188
    and great-power conflict,
      191–194, 196
    middle powers' partners in,
      194–195
    and national security, 172
    of newly-democratized
      Canadian government,
      95–96
    political, 38–39, 154, 170
    popular, 94
    and posture of
      inoffensiveness, 173–174
    in presidential systems,
      119–120
    privileges of, 20*n*

Index